SEAN JAY

The Great British Cheesecake Cookbook

This book was professionally typeset on Reedsy.
Find out more at reedsy.com

Contents

1

Introduction

Welcome to the tasty journey of cheesecake creation! My venture into the world of cheesecakes began in 2016, armed with an insatiable appetite for gorgeous desserts and a determination to conquer the art of baking. Little did I know that my initial foray into fridge-set cheesecakes would be an amusing lesson in dessert resilience.

At my food market debut at a 'happened-once-and-never-happened-again' location in West London, I had a number of gelatine-set beauties adorning my display... several of which dramatically fell apart in a big wet mess upon liberation from their moulds. It was a scene that could rival a baking disaster reality show, but it marked the turning point in my cheesecake chronicles.

Enter the more resilient 'New York style' baked cheesecakes – robust, dependable, and a hit among the discerning food market patrons of London. These baked wonders not only weathered warmer days but also outsold their delicate fridge-set counterparts.

So, in a surprisingly short period of time, the fridge-set

cheesecakes were gracefully phased out, making way for the triumphant reign of their baked brethren. It became evident that the comforting familiarity of baked cheesecakes resonated with customers, many of whom had encountered these delights during their travels abroad, particularly whilst in the USA.

And now, I present my cheesecake compendium to you. This collection of recipes is a testament to countless trials, satisfied customers, and the sweet success that comes from embracing the charm of baked cheesecakes. Each recipe has undergone rigorous testing, ensuring a symphony of flavors that will dance on your taste buds.

As you embark on your cheesecake-making adventure, remember that my journey began with little culinary prowess, barely extending beyond reheating a pizza. If I can evolve from a pizza reheater to a cheesecake connoisseur, rest assured, so can you. So, buckle up, dear reader, and let the cheesecake-making escapades unfold – deliciously.

Happy baking!

Sean Jay

2

Necessary Equipment

Before you embark on your cheesecake journey, let's make sure you have the essential tools to create these delectable delights. Here's a rundown of the necessary equipment:

Tins

Each recipe in this book is tailored for a 9-inch springform tin, or 23cm if you prefer. Invest in a sturdy non-stick tin or two. I recommend Circulon for quality and durability, mainly because I tried this particular brand once, it worked well, and I stuck with it. A 9-inch tin produces cheesecakes generous enough for twelve or perfect for sharing with friends. Don't worry if you're baking for one; these baked wonders last up to ten days in the fridge.

Speaking of which, the recipes given in this book are designed specifically for this size of cake. And these are very big cakes.

If you fancy something smaller, simply reduce each recipe by 25% and don't worry too much about being exact. The cheesecakes will still turn out well. You can even reduce each recipe by half, should your tins be 4 or 5 inches in diameter.

Again, don't worry: these recipes are pretty much foolproof and were developed following many catastrophes in the kitchen which I had to put right.

Non-stick spray

An important purchase to ensure your cheesecakes don't stick to the sides. Most non-stick tins lose their charm after a couple of bakes, so I recommend using 'Release-a-Cake' spray by PME, easily available online and at all good cookery shops. A small investment for a smoother baking experience. If, however, you've picked this book up literally 30 seconds before baking, greasing the sides of your tin with unsalted butter will work nicely.

9-inch round silicone papers

These are essential for the base of the tin. While you can use the non-stick spray mentioned earlier, using silicone papers keeps the biscuit base dry, ensuring a perfect foundation for your cheesecake creation.

If you (naturally) don't want to buy 100 of these at a time, then simple baking paper, cut to fit will also suffice.

Simply remove the base of your Sprinform tin, lay it on top of your baking paper, grab a pencil and draw around the circumference of the base. Then cut around this and voila! You have your own silicone paper base onto which you can place your biscuit base.

Bowl and mixer

Whether handheld or standing, opt for an electric mixer – it's your ally in achieving the perfect cheesecake consistency. Leave the manual beating for those looking for a workout, not for crafting delicate desserts. I've successfully made cheesecakes over the years with both handheld and standing mixers so don't worry which one you have.

Food processor

A time-saver for blitzing those biscuit crumbs. If you're feeling old-school, you can always go for the rolling pin method, but why exert extra effort when a food processor can do the job efficiently?

Tin foil and cling film

Get ready for a Bain-Marie baking adventure! Wrapping your cheesecake in cling film and tin foil ensures it stays dry and delicious during the baking process. A watertight strategy to prevent your cheesecake from taking an unscheduled swim. I talk about exactly how to do this in detail in the section, 'How to bake your cheesecake'.

Large tin for Bain-Marie

You're going to need a large baking tray that has a depth of a couple of inches so that you can then create a Bain-Marie in which your cheesecake can cook. Simply, this is the type of baking tray that you would usually cook a roast chicken in, with a depth of maybe 4 or 5 inches.

Now that you've got your arsenal of baking tools, you're all set to dive into the world of cheesecake creation. Get ready for a delightful journey of mixing, baking, and savoring the sweet rewards!

3

How to spray and line your tins

Ah, the mysterious ritual of spraying and lining a tin – a rite of passage for anyone transitioning from pizza reheating to the delicate art of baking. Do not worry: like all things in baking, it's actually simple.

Spraying and lining are your culinary security blankets, ensuring your creation gracefully exits the springfrom tin without sticking.

Spraying:

Think of this as giving your tin a mini spa day. Grab a can of non-stick spray, preferably the 'Release-a-Cake' spray mentioned previously. Spritz it generously, around the inside of the tin's sides, ensuring every nook and cranny gets a fine mist. Picture it as the tin's way of putting on a silky baking sunscreen – protection against any sticky cheesecake

Lining:

Now, the lining is like providing a cozy bed for your cheesecake to rest upon. It's best to use the precut 9 inch/23cm silicone circles, available in all good kitchen shops. Or, as mentioned previously, create your own from simple shop-bought baking paper. Place it at the bottom, ensuring a snug fit. This lining ensures your cheesecake can easily slip out, just like a pizza from a well-floured peel. No sticking, no drama. Just smooth baking.

In essence, spraying and lining are the unsung heroes of your baking escapade. They ensure your creation pops out effortlessly. So, embrace the spray, befriend the lining, and let your cheesecake creation unfold like the culinary masterpiece it's destined to be.

4

How to bake your cheesecake

When it comes to nailing the art of baking cheesecakes, the go-to move is the Bain-Marie method. Picture this – your cheesecake cozily baking in its springform tin, taking a warm bath in a large roasting tin with a nice supply of water. The water should hug your tin about two-thirds of the way up, preventing any burning mishaps.

Now, let's dive into the wild world of oven temperatures, where each oven has its own quirks and charms.

In my first kitchen, located in my tiny flat in London, complete with a humble home oven, 170°C was the magic number. That one had a single fan, so it took its sweet time, but the cheese-cakes baked perfectly. In fact, I still think that, several ovens on, this one cooked the cakes better than any of the more expensive machines we sourced later.

As the business grew, I purchased a countertop oven – small but packing a punch with two fans. Here's the catch: anything hotter than 140°C turned into a cheesecake nightmare. Burnt edges and occasional cracks – talk about kitchen drama. So I had to be very careful with this machine, with each cake taking no more than an hour at most. Good for speed, not so good for culinary perfection.

As the cheesecake business expanded, a German titan entered the scene – a professional Rational oven that could bake twenty cheesecakes at once. This beast liked things at a precise 135°C, ensuring a symphony of perfectly baked cheesecakes.

So, here's the kitchen wisdom: every oven has a unique character with its own range of temperatures. Whether it's 170°C, 110°C, or 135°C, finding that sweet spot takes some experimenting. Start at 170°C in your home oven and see where the cheesecake journey takes you. Embrace the oven quirks, enjoy the variations, and let your cheesecakes shine as the kitchen maestros they were born to be.

So long as you keep your eye on things, and don't allow the cake to burn, it's not really possible to get it wrong. And whilst the baking of the cheesecake is a very important part of the creation process, allowing the eggs to coagulate, setting the cake in the fridge afterwards goes a long way towards the firmness of your creation. In essence, the cake is cooked once it is firm on top, but still wobbles in the middle. If you have a food thermometer, the cake is cooked once the centre reaches 75°C or higher, so don't be scared to stab it in the middle and see how it's doing.

5

The Bain Marie

In everyday cooking, the Bain-Marie is a practical technique that comes in handy when working with delicate dishes such as cheesecakes.

A Bain-Marie is simply a large tin filled with simmering water, providing indirect heat to your cheesecake, which cooks inside it's carefully wrapped Springform tin. This technique ensures a gradual and gentle cooking process. It's like having a practical assistant in the kitchen, shielding your dish from direct oven heat. The goal is straightforward – steady and even cooking without burning.

Naturally, you must wrap your Springform tin in clingfilm and silver foil to ensure that the water does not get into your cake. The best method I have found involves using strong silver foil. Wrap the outside of your Springform tin in one strong piece of silver foil, scrunching it right up to the top of the sides of the tin. Then wrap the outside of the tin again, this time in clingfilm. Then add another layer of silver foil on top of this. If any water manages to get into your cake following this threefold layering technique, I'd be amazed.

There are also companies that are now making silicone moulds into which you can simply place your Sprinform tin. I bought some lovely yellow moulds from the Easy Bath Cheesecake Wrap Company, based in the USA. This really does save valuable time in the kitchen and absolutely ensures that water has no chance of getting into your cake.

When it's time to bake your cake, the best thing to do is this:

Your cheesecake has been poured into your Sprinform tin. The tin itself has been wrapped in silver foil, clingfilm and then another layer of silver foil, as described above. Place the cake in the large, empty roasting tin that will become your Bain-Marie and put them both on a shelf in the middle of your pre-heated oven. Then, using water from a recently boiled kettle, fill up the tin with near boiling water until it is two-thirds of the way up the tin. No higher (don't tempt fate) and not too much lower, unless you prefer your cheesecake to be a little more toasty (and some people do).

Close the oven door, and let the Bain-Marie work its magic. This method ensures reliable and consistent results without any culinary theatrics.

When your creation is ready, it should come out perfectly cooked. The Bain-Marie, a reliable kitchen companion, has quietly contributed to the success of your dish. So, embrace this straightforward technique – let the Bain-Marie be your practical ally in the kitchen.

6

Cracking Up?

Cheesecakes can develop cracks for several reasons, and addressing these factors is key to achieving a smoother result. I have had a few cakes crack on me over the years, and the major culprits are as follows:

1. High Oven Temperature

- Adjust your oven temperature according to your recipe to prevent the cheesecake from cooking too quickly on the outside. This adjustment helps reduce the risk of cracks. Follow the recommended temperature and baking time. Slow and steady wins the race. The cake should 'puff up' nicely as it reaches the final stages of baking.

2. Insufficient Tin Coating

- Ensure the springform tin is thoroughly coated with Release-a-Cake spray before adding the biscuit base and filling. Proper coating facilitates easy release and minimizes sticking, reducing the likelihood of cracks.

3. Bain-Marie Technique

- All the recipes in this book require the cheesecakes to be baked in a Bain-Marie. This method provides gentle and even heat distribution, minimizing the risk of cracks. The water bath creates a moist environment, preventing the cheesecake from drying out and cracking.

Additionally, it's worth noting that opening the oven door fully, in my opinion, makes no significant difference. While it's recommended to open the oven door slightly at first once the cake has cooked, allowing the cake to continue cooking indirectly in its Bain-Marie, I've found that taking cheesecakes directly out of the oven and placing them on a cooling rack has never once led to cracking. This suggests that a gradual cooling process may not be as crucial in preventing cracks as some might think.

Indeed, when things got very busy in the commercial kitchen, it was not unusual for us to remove boiling hot cheesecakes from the oven, only to have them cooling in a Blastchiller ten minutes later. Within an hour, the cakes were down to 2°C. Without any cracks. So exposing hot cheesecakes to cold air immediately following cooking does not cause cracks.

In addition, overbeating a cheesecake batter, especially when working with cream cheese, can contribute to cracks and splits in the final product. Here's why:

1. Incorporating Too Much Air

- Overbeating introduces excessive air into the batter. Air pockets in the cheesecake mixture can expand during baking and cause the cake to rise excessively. As the cheesecake cools, these expanded pockets collapse, leaving behind gaps that manifest as cracks. So; once the eggs are incorporated into the mixture, stop beating!

2. Structural Impact on Cream Cheese

- Cream cheese, a key ingredient in cheesecake, is a delicate structure of fats and proteins. Overbeating can disrupt this structure, leading to a less stable batter. When baked, an unstable batter is more prone to developing cracks and splits as it sets.

3. Overmixing Causes Uneven Baking

- Overbeating can result in an overly smooth and thin batter. During baking, this uniform consistency may lead to uneven heat distribution, causing certain areas of the cheesecake to cook faster than others. This imbalance can contribute to cracks as the cheesecake cools.

To avoid cracks and splits, it's crucial to mix the cheesecake batter up until the point at which the ingredients are combined and smooth. Be mindful of incorporating air and disrupting the structure of the cream cheese. Opt for a gentle and controlled mixing approach to ensure a creamy, stable, and crack-free cheesecake.

Experimentation with these factors can help you find the best approach for your cheesecake baking endeavors.

7

Troubleshooting

Indeed, making cheesecakes can be a delicate process, but the good news is that most issues are fixable. Whether it's a cracked surface, uneven texture, or other hiccups, adjustments in ingredients, baking techniques, or even creative toppings can often turn things around. Don't be discouraged by minor setbacks; instead, consider them opportunities to enhance your cheesecake-making skills and create a dessert that's uniquely yours.

1. Moisture on top of the cake forming following refrigeration

- If you find moisture on top of your cheesecake, don't worry! Simply use one or two pieces of kitchen towel to gently dab away until the cake's surface is completely dry. Avoid attempting to add toppings to a wet cheesecake, as they might slide off. This quick fix ensures a dry and stable surface, making it easier for your chosen toppings to stick, enhancing the overall presentation of your delicious cheesecake.

2. Cake not releasing well

- Always ensure that you are very liberal with the Cake Release Spray.
- Over time, your springform tin will lose it's natural non-stick ability. So the cake release spray is a must, but you can also use a chef's blowtorch and go quickly around the edges of the tin. Watch how easily your cake falls out! If you don't have a blowtorch, a kitchen towel, soaked in hot water, and wrapped around the edges of your cheesecakes tin for 30 seconds or so will also help to release the cake with greater ease.

3. Lumps in the cream cheese mix

- Sometimes, we don't have time to allow the cream cheese we have bought to 'come to room temperature'. When you then attempt to mix this with the other ingredients, lumps may well form that seem impossible to get rid of. There is an easy solution to this: simply fill your kitchen sink with very hot water, and plunge your mixing bowl into it. Give it. a few minutes, and then stir the cream cheese mix with a spatula or wooden spoon. The lumps will have almost entirely disappeared.

4. Sugar, flour and other ingredients getting stuck to the bottom of the bowl

- As Mary Berry always advises, make sure you scrape down the sides of the mixing bowl with a spatula and always check the bottom of the bowl. This is where sugar and flour can often become lodged and you may not realise this until you go to pour the mix onto your cheesecake base, by which time, it is is technically too late to rescue.

- If this does happen however, do not panic. If the biscuit base has set properly, it should still be cold enough and you can scrape the cheesecake mix back into the bowl and mix it again, this time ensuring all the ingredients are fully incorporated.

5 . Cakes with biscuit toppings

- These include the Oreo and Lotus Biscoff cheesecakes. Cook these slowly and evenly, because it takes time for the heat to penetrate through the biscuit topping.
- Too hot, too soon, will likely result in cracks appearing. So take the temperature down, and take your time.

8

CLASSIC ENGLISH VANILLA

Embark on a delightful baking adventure with the most classic of cheesecakes, a blend of British tradition and New York flair that promises to be the highlight of your culinary escapades.

In the heart of this baking journey lies the meticulous selection of ingredients. We will be carefully infusing the batter with the finest vanilla extract, blending it harmoniously with rich cream cheese and eggs. Each step is an ode to precision, ensuring that every bite unfolds a symphony of flavors that captures the essence of culinary simplicity.

As your kitchen transforms into a haven of aromas, visualize the velvety texture of the cheesecake coming to life in your oven. The delicate balance of sweetness and richness will enchant your senses, making the anticipation of that first bite all the more thrilling.

But the baking adventure doesn't end there. Picture adorning each slice with the vibrant allure of juicy strawberries, their freshness adding a burst of flavor to the decadent layers beneath. And for an extra layer of indulgence, consider a dollop of whipped cream, turning every forkful into a heavenly escape.

For those who appreciate the beauty of unadorned simplicity, relish the classic cheesecake straight from the oven. Let it stand alone as a testament to the joy of baking, an iconic treat that brings a burst of delight with every freshly baked bite.

So, preheat that oven, gather your ingredients, and let the aroma of our classic cheesecake turn your baking day into an unforgettable journey of sweet indulgence.

Base
    260g digestive biscuits
    90g unsalted butter
    10g caster sugar

Filling
    900g Cream Cheese
    300ml double cream
    1 tin condensed milk
    40g caster sugar
    1 tsp vanilla extract
    35g plain flour
    4 eggs

Instructions:

1. Prepare the Biscuits

- Place the digestive biscuits in a food processor.
- Pulse the biscuits into fine crumbs.

2. Melt the Butter

- In a saucepan or microwave-safe bowl, melt the unsalted butter.

3. Combine Biscuits and Butter

- In the food processor, combine the biscuit crumbs with the caster sugar. Add the melted butter to this mixture.

4. Mix Thoroughly

- Blitz the ingredients together for a few seconds until the biscuit crumbs are evenly coated with the melted butter and sugar. The mixture should resemble damp sand.

5. Prepare the Tin

- Take a 9-inch springform tin, which should be sprayed and lined.
- Pour the biscuit mixture into the base of the tin, and spread it out evenly, using a fork. Use the back of a spoon or the bottom of a glass to compact the mixture. Keep the pressure light but firm.

6. Chill the Base

- Place the tin in the refrigerator and let the base chill for 20 minutes or so. This helps the butter solidify, creating a firm foundation for your cheesecake.

7. Preheat the Oven

- Preheat your oven to 170°C.

8. Prepare the Cream Cheese and Double Cream

- In a large mixing bowl, place the cream cheese. Ensure it's at room temperature for smoother blending. If at all possible, buy your cream cheese the day before baking, and leave it out of the refrigerator overnight. Add the double cream to the cream cheese.

9. Add the Condensed Milk

- Open the tin of condensed milk and add it to the cream cheese.

10. Incorporate Sugar

- Sprinkle the caster sugar into the bowl with the cream cheese and condensed milk.

11. Add Vanilla Extract

- Add the teaspoon of vanilla extract to the mixture.

12. Sift in Flour

- Sift the plain flour into the bowl to avoid any lumps in the filling.

13. Blend Smoothly

- Use a hand mixer or a stand mixer to blend the ingredients together. Mix until the texture is smooth and all ingredients are well combined. Ensure there are no lumps.

14. Add the eggs

- Add the eggs, preferably one at a time, and scraping down the sides as you go, ensuring any unmixed ingredients are incorporated into the mix.

15. Pour onto the Base

- Once your cheesecake base has chilled, pour the cream cheese filling onto it, spreading it evenly, smoothing the top with a spoon.

16. Wrap and Bake

- Wrap the tin in silver foil, then clingfilm, then sliver foil, as per my suggestion in the Bain Marie section of this book.
- Bake at 170°C for an hour, or until golden brown on top but still wobbly in the centre. Once it reaches it's optimum state of being cooked, the cake should 'puff up' above the top of the tin, something that will drop as soon as you take the cake out of the oven. If you feel it requires longer, give it a little more time in the oven.

17. Cool and Chill

- After baking, open the oven door and allow the cheesecake to cool slightly. When ready, remove it from the oven and the Bain Marie, and allow it to cool to room temperature, preferably on a wire rack.

- Cover and refrigerate for at least eight hours, or preferably overnight before serving.

9

SALTED CARAMEL

Step into the realm of irresistible indulgence with our gooey salted caramel cheesecake – a true crowd-pleaser that stands among our enduring favorites. Picture this decadent creation baked to perfection, its luscious layers waiting to delight your taste buds.

But the magic doesn't end there. Envision an additional layer of sumptuous salted caramel generously drizzled atop the cheesecake once it's set. This is not just a dessert; it's a journey into the world of unparalleled indulgence.

Allow your kitchen to transform into a haven of rich aromas as the cheesecake bakes, each moment building anticipation for the gooey goodness that awaits. Picture the velvety texture and the perfect balance of sweetness meeting the delightful saltiness, creating a symphony of flavors that will leave you craving more.

Now, let's delve into the intriguing story behind this extraordinary dessert. Imagine a renowned cake vlogger, unable to contain the delight inspired by our salted caramel cheesecake, letting out an unexpected exclamation of joy live on television. A flavorful expletive, if you will, that spoke volumes about the sheer irresistibility of this indulgent treat. And fear not, he not only retained his job but became a true ambassador for the enchanting allure of our gooey salted caramel creation.

The charm of this cheesecake lies in its audacious ability to push the boundaries of decadence. It doesn't just satisfy your sweet tooth; it leaves a lasting impression on even the most seasoned dessert enthusiasts. It's a dessert adventure, an exploration of flavors that will make every bite a celebration of culinary delight.

So, as you embark on the baking journey of our gooey salted caramel cheesecake, envision each step as a pathway to extraordinary taste. Picture the smiles of satisfaction as your creation graces the table, leaving an indelible mark on the hearts and palates of those lucky enough to indulge in its gooey goodness.

Base
260g digestive biscuits
90g unsalted butter
10g caster sugar

Filling
900g Cream Cheese
250ml double cream
180g dark brown sugar
100g light brown sugar
100g tinned caramel
3 pinches sea salt flakes
45g plain flour
4 eggs

Topping

1/2 gelatine sheet.
50g dark brown sugar
1 pinch sea salt flakes
50ml double cream
50g caramel

Instructions:

1. Prepare the Biscuits

- Place the digestive biscuits in a food processor.
- Pulse until the biscuits into fine crumbs.

2. Melt the Butter

- In a saucepan or microwave-safe bowl, melt the unsalted butter.

3. Combine Biscuits and Butter

- In the food processor, combine the biscuit crumbs with the caster sugar. Add the melted butter to this mixture.

4. Mix Thoroughly

- Blitz the ingredients together for a few seconds until the biscuit crumbs are evenly coated with the melted butter and sugar. The mixture should resemble damp sand.

5. Prepare the Tin

- Take a 9-inch springform tin, which should be sprayed and lined.
- Pour the biscuit mixture into the base of the tin, and spread it out evenly, using a fork. Use the back of a spoon or the bottom of a glass to compact the mixture. Keep the pressure light but firm.

6. Chill the Base

- Place the tin in the refrigerator and let the base chill for 20 minutes or so. This helps the butter solidify, creating a firm foundation for your cheesecake.

7. Preheat the Oven

- Preheat your oven to 170°C.

8. Prepare the Cream Cheese

- In a large mixing bowl, place the cream cheese. Ensure it's at room temperature for smoother blending. If at all possible, buy your cream cheese the day before baking, and leave it out of the refrigerator overnight. Add the double cream to the cream cheese.

9. Add the dark brown and light brown sugar

- Add both quantities of sugar to the cream cheese in the mixing bowl.

10. Incorporate Caramel

- Add 100g of Caramel to the mix.

11. Add Sea Salt

- Add three generous pinches of Sea Salt.

12. Sift in Flour

- Sift the plain flour into the bowl to avoid any lumps in the filling.

13. Blend Smoothly

- Use a hand mixer or a stand mixer to blend the ingredients together. Mix until the texture is smooth and all ingredients are well combined. Ensure there are no lumps.

14. Add the eggs

- Add the eggs, preferably one at a time, and scraping down the sides as you go, ensuring any unmixed ingredients are incorporated into the mix.

15. Pour onto the Base

- Once your cheesecake base has chilled, pour the cream cheese filling onto it, spreading it evenly, smoothing the top with a spoon.

16. Wrap and Bake

- Wrap the tin in silver foil, then clingfilm, then sliver foil, as per my suggestion in the Bain Marie section of this book.
- Bake at 170°C for an hour and ten minutes, or until nicely brown on top but still wobbly in the centre. Once it reaches it's optimum state of being cooked, the cake should 'puff up' above the top of the tin, something that will drop as soon as you take the cake out of the oven. If you feel it requires longer, give it a little more time in the oven.

17. Cool and Chill

- After baking, open the oven door and allow the cheesecake to cool slightly. When ready, remove it from the oven and the Bain Marie, and allow it to cool to room temperature.
- Cover and refrigerate for at least eight hours, or preferably overnight before preparing the topping.

18. Preparing the topping

- Prepare the Gelatine by soaking the gelatine sheet in cold water according to package instructions until it becomes soft and pliable.
- In a saucepan, mix together dark brown sugar, a pinch of sea salt flakes, double cream, and caramel. Heat the mixture over low-medium heat, stirring continuously until the sugar dissolves and the ingredients blend into a smooth consistency.
- Squeeze any excess water from the soaked gelatine sheet and add it to the mixture. Stir until the gelatine dissolves completely, contributing to the setting of the topping.
- Allow the topping mixture to cool slightly before pouring

it over the baked and set cheesecake. This step ensures a smooth and even distribution of the topping.

· Place the cheesecake with the topping back into the refrig-erator to allow it to set completely. This should only take an hour or so, before the cake is ready to serve.

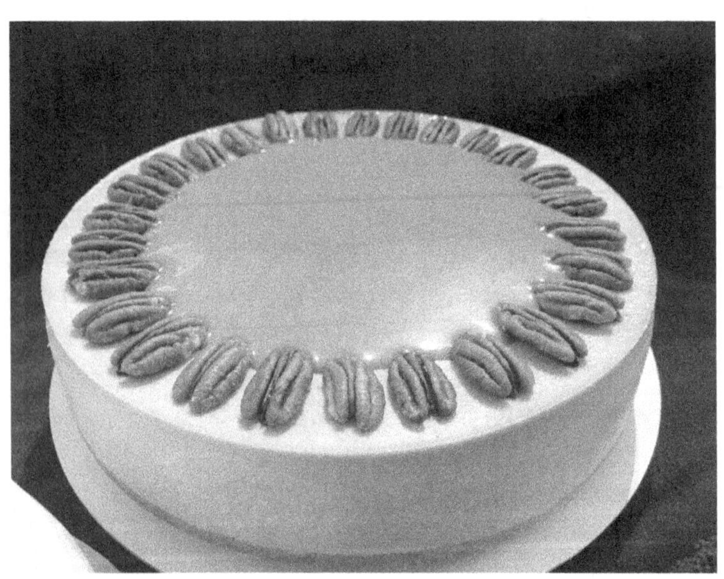

10

LEMON MERINGUE

Embark on a delightful baking escapade with our fabulously tangy Lemon Meringue Cheesecake – a creation that transcends the ordinary and elevates your culinary experience to new heights. This enchanting dessert, a true labor of love, is not just a treat but a pleasant companion on warm summer days.

Picture the beginning of this culinary adventure: a biscuit base meticulously slathered in zesty lemon curd, setting the stage for a symphony of flavors to unfold. As you dive into the process, envision the luscious lemon cheesecake mix cascading over the lemony base, each layer contributing to the tantalizing complexity of this indulgent creation.

But we don't stop there. Imagine the final act as the cheesecake emerges from the oven, perfectly baked and set. Now, the grand finale: a gloriously glossy meringue, spooned generously on top. And here comes the chef's torch, delicately browning the meringue to perfection, with a touch of drama and a careful eye to avoid setting any eyebrows on fire.

This dessert is more than just a subdued indulgence; it's a refreshing burst of citrus sunshine on a plate. It's the perfect companion for lazy summer afternoons, a sweet respite that doesn't demand grandiose descriptions or culinary theatrics. The Lemon Meringue Cheesecake, in its simplicity, invites you to savor the essence of summer – a moment of pure delight with each decadent forkful.

So, gather your ingredients, preheat that oven, and envision the aroma of lemony goodness wafting through your kitchen. As you embark on the journey of baking our Lemon Meringue Cheesecake, may each step be a celebration of the vibrant flavors that make summer desserts truly unforgettable.

Base
260g digestive biscuits
90g unsalted butter
10g caster sugar
1tbsp lemon curd

Filling
800g Cream Cheese
200g double cream
1tsp vanilla extract
80g caster sugar
2 lemons zest & juice
30g plain flour
3 eggs

Topping
3 egg whites
150g caster sugar
1 tbsp water
1/2tsp cream of tartar

Instructions:

1. Prepare the Biscuits

- Place the digestive biscuits in a food processor.
- Pulse the biscuits into fine crumbs.

2. Melt the Butter

- In a saucepan or microwave-safe bowl, melt the unsalted butter.

3. Combine Biscuits and Butter

- In the food processor, combine the biscuit crumbs with the caster sugar. Add the melted butter to this mixture.

4. Mix Thoroughly

- Blitz the ingredients together for a few seconds, until the biscuit crumbs are evenly coated with the melted butter and sugar. The mixture should resemble damp sand.

5. Prepare the Tin

- Take a 9-inch springform tin, which should be sprayed and lined.
- Pour the biscuit mixture into the base of the tin, and spread it out evenly, using a fork. Use the back of a spoon or the bottom of a glass to compact the mixture. Keep the pressure light but firm.

6. Chill the Base

- Place the tin in the refrigerator and let the base chill for 20 minutes or so. This helps the butter solidify, creating a firm foundation for your cheesecake. Once firm, use a spoon to slather the lemon curd over the bottom of the biscuit base.

7. Preheat the Oven

- Preheat your oven to 170°C.

8. Prepare the Cream Cheese

- In a large mixing bowl, place the cream cheese. Ensure it's at room temperature for smoother blending. If at all possible, buy your cream cheese the day before baking, and leave it out of the refrigerator overnight. Add the double cream to the cream cheese.

9. Add the vanilla extract

- Add the vanilla extract to the cream cheese in the mixing bowl.

10. Incorporate the sugar

- Add the 80g of Caster Sugar to the mix.

11. Add Lemon Zest and Juice

- Start this process by adding the zest of two lemons into the bowl. Do this using a food grater. Once done, squeeze both lemons and incorporate their juice into the mix, ensuring no pips end up in the cheesecake.

12. Sift in Flour

- Sift the plain flour into the bowl to avoid any lumps in the filling.

13. Blend Smoothly

- Use a hand mixer or a stand mixer to blend the ingredients together. Mix until the texture is smooth and all ingredients are well combined. Ensure there are no lumps.

14. Add the eggs

- Add the three eggs, preferably one at a time, and scraping down the sides as you go, ensuring any unmixed ingredients are incorporated into the mix.

15. Pour onto the Base

- Once your cheesecake base has chilled and the lemon curd has set, pour the cream cheese filling onto it, spreading it evenly, smoothing the top with a spoon.

16. Wrap and Bake

- Wrap the tin in silver foil, then clingfilm, then sliver foil, as per my suggestion in the Bain Marie section of this book.

- Bake at 160°C for an hour, or until nicely brown on top but still wobbly in the centre. Once it reaches it's optimum state of being cooked, the cake should 'puff up' above the top of the tin, something that will drop as soon as you take the cake out of the oven. If you feel it requires longer, give it a little more time in the oven.

17. Cool and Chill

- After baking, open the oven door and allow the cheesecake to cool slightly. When ready, remove it from the oven and the Bain Marie, and allow it to cool to room temperature.
- Cover and refrigerate for at least eight hours, or preferably overnight before preparing the topping.

18. Preparing the Italian Meringue Topping

- The make the meringue, combine the sugar, cream of tartar, tablespoon of water and egg whites in a large bowl, and place this over a pot of simmering water.
- Beat using an electric mixer on a steady speed until the sugar has dissolved and the egg whites are warm. This should take about five minutes.
- Remove the bowl from the heat, and continue to beat the egg white mixture on a higher speed, until stiff, glossy peaks form. Make sure they are nice and solid.
- Add the Italian Meringue to the top of the cheesecake in a flat dome shape.
- Then, use a kitchen blowtorch to toast the outside of the meringue.
- Place the cheesecake back in the fridge until you are ready

to serve.

11

OREOS

Embark on a layered journey with my Oreo Cheesecake – a union of two distinct cheesecakes harmonizing in every bite. Picture the decadence: a chocolate digestive base, a sturdy foundation for the symphony of flavors that unfolds.

Atop this canvas, a velvety vanilla buttercream cheesecake layer adds a subtle richness, a gentle precursor to the indulgence that follows. Enter the Oreo layer – a fusion of creamy cheesecake mixed with the iconic Oreo cookie, creating a dance of textures and tastes.

To crown this masterpiece, we liberally sprinkle Oreo crumbs over the top. Why? Because the allure of Oreos is timeless, and in this duo, there's an acknowledgment that one can never have enough of these irresistible delights.

This Oreo Cheesecake Duo is not just a dessert; it's an exploration of layers, a delightful narrative that invites you to savor each nuance. With every bite, it's a reminder that the combination of chocolate, vanilla, and the beloved Oreo is a culinary harmony worth celebrating.

Base
    250g digestive biscuits
    90g unsalted butter
    10g caster sugar
    15g cocoa powder

Buttercream Cheesecake Filling
    700g Cream Cheese
    110g caster sugar
    1tsp vanilla extract
    20g plain flour
    3 eggs

Oreo Cheesecake Filling
    500g Cream Cheese
    100g caster sugar
    20g plain flour
    2 eggs
    150g Oreos, blitzed to crumbs

Topping
    100g blitzed Oreos

Instructions:

1. Prepare the Biscuits

- Place the digestive biscuits in a food processor.
- Pulse the biscuits into fine crumbs.

2. Melt the Butter

- In a saucepan or microwave-safe bowl, melt the unsalted butter.

3. Combine Biscuits, Sugar, Cocoa Powder and Butter

- In the food processor, combine the biscuit crumbs with the caster sugar and the cocoa powder, giving it a brief blitz to ensure everything is combined. Add the melted butter to this mixture.

4. Mix Thoroughly

- Blitz the ingredients together for a few seconds until the biscuit crumbs are evenly coated with the melted butter, cocoa powder and sugar. The mixture should resemble damp sand.

5. Prepare the Tin

- Take a 9-inch springform tin, which should be sprayed and lined.
- Pour the biscuit mixture into the base of the tin, and spread it out evenly, using a fork. Use the back of a spoon or the bottom of a glass to compact the mixture. Keep the pressure light but firm.

6. Chill the Base

- Place the tin in the refrigerator and let the base chill for 20 minutes or so. This helps the butter solidify, creating a firm foundation for your cheesecake.

7. Preheat the Oven

- Preheat your oven to 170°C.

8. Prepare the Cream Cheese for the Buttercream Cheesecake Layer

- In a large mixing bowl, place the 700g of cream cheese. Ensure it's at room temperature for smoother blending. If at all possible, buy your cream cheese the day before baking, and leave it out of the refrigerator overnight.

9. Add the sugar, vanilla extract and flour.

- Add these ingredients to the cream cheese, and mix them together until smooth.

10. Incorporate the eggs

- Add the 3 eggs, preferably one at a time, and scraping down the sides as you go, ensuring any unmixed ingredients are incorporated into the mix.

11. Pour onto the base

- Once your chocolate cheesecake base has chilled, pour the cream cheese filling onto it, spreading it evenly. Put this back in the fridge to allow it to set a little.

12. Prepare the Oreo Cheesecake Layer

- In another large mixing bowl, place the 500g of cream cheese. Ensure it's at room temperature for smoother blending. Add the sugar and flour and blend together.

13. Add the Oreos to the mix

- Blitz 150g of Oreos in your food processor. Then add these to the cheesecake mix. Use a hand mixer or a stand mixer to blend the ingredients together. Mix until the texture is smooth and all ingredients are well combined.

14. Add the 2 eggs

- Add the eggs, preferably one at a time, and scraping down the sides as you go, ensuring any unmixed ingredients are incorporated into the mix.

15. Pour onto the Base

- Once again, remove the Springform tin from the fridge, and spread the Oreo cream cheese filling on top of the Buttercream cheesecake layer, spreading it evenly, smoothing the top with a spoon.

16. Blitz Oreos for the Topping

- Take 100g of Oreos and blitz them roughly in the food processor. Then, using a dessert spoon, spread these evenly over the top of the Oreo Cheesecake layer, a spoonful at a time.

17. Wrap and Bake

- Wrap the tin in silver foil, then clingfilm, then sliver foil, as per my suggestion in the Bain Marie section of this book.
- Bake at 150°C for an hour and a half. This cheesecake takes longer than others, as the Oreo topping means the heat requires more time to penetrate and cook the interior of the cake. Once it reaches it's optimum state of being cooked, the cake should 'puff up' above the top of the tin, something that will drop as soon as you take the cake out of the oven. If you feel it requires longer, give it a little more time in the oven.

18. Cool and Chill

- After baking, open the oven door and allow the cheesecake to cool slightly. When ready, remove it from the oven and the Bain Marie, and allow it to cool to room temperature, preferably on a wire rack.
- Cover and refrigerate for at least eight hours, or preferably overnight before serving.

12

MANGO & PASSIONFRUIT

Immerse yourself in the summer allure with our Mango Passion Cheesecake, a perennial favorite that effortlessly captures the essence of sun-soaked days. Envision the creation of this culinary masterpiece, where a velvety cheesecake is infused with the lusciousness of fresh mango, promising a celebration of tropical sweetness in every sumptuous bite.

Visualize the grandeur of this indulgence: a vibrant layer of tangy passion fruit crowning the cheesecake. This zesty twist is the pièce de résistance, a tantalizing dance of flavors harmonizing seamlessly with the underlying mango goodness. It's a tropical flavor extravaganza, a sensory journey that infuses any occasion with the vibrant spirit of faraway shores.

As your kitchen becomes a tropical oasis, imagine the aroma of fresh mango permeating the air, mingling with the exotic notes of passion fruit. Feel the anticipation build with each carefully crafted layer, knowing that the final result will be a decadent escape into the essence of summer.

But this cheesecake is more than just a dessert; it's your ticket to a momentary escape. With every forkful, savor the warmth of summer encapsulated in the delightful union of mango and passion fruit. Let the Mango Passion Cheesecake be the centerpiece of your gathering, a sweet indulgence that invites you and your guests to revel in the blissful allure of sun-kissed flavors.

So, gather your ingredients, and let the Mango Passion Cheesecake transport you to a tropical paradise. May each bite be a celebration of the vibrant and exotic, bringing the taste of summer to every delightful moment.

Base
  260g digestive biscuits
  90g unsalted butter
  10g caster sugar

Filling
  900g Cream Cheese
  300ml double cream
  100ml Mango puree
  140g caster sugar
  15g plain flour
  4 eggs

Topping
  1 gelatine strip
  3 Passionfruit, sliced and scooped
  25g mango purée
  30g caster sugar
  3 Passionfruit pulp

Instructions:

1. Prepare the Biscuits

- Place the digestive biscuits in a food processor.
- Pulse until the biscuits turn into fine crumbs.

2. Melt the Butter

- In a saucepan or microwave-safe bowl, melt the unsalted butter.

3. Combine Biscuits and Butter

- In the food processor, combine the biscuit crumbs with the caster sugar. Add the melted butter to this mixture.

4. Mix Thoroughly

- Blitz the ingredients together until the biscuit crumbs are evenly coated with the melted butter and sugar. The mixture should resemble damp sand.

5. Prepare the Tin

- Take a 9-inch springform tin, which should be sprayed and lined.
- Pour the biscuit mixture into the base of the tin, and spread it out evenly, using a fork. Use the back of a spoon or the bottom of a glass to compact the mixture. Keep the pressure light but firm.

6. Chill the Base

- Place the tin in the refrigerator and let the base chill for 20 minutes or so. This helps the butter solidify, creating a firm foundation for your cheesecake.

7. Preheat the Oven

- Preheat your oven to 170°C.

8. Prepare the Cream Cheese

- In a large mixing bowl, place the cream cheese. Ensure it's at room temperature for smoother blending. If at all possible, buy your cream cheese the day before baking, and leave it out of the refrigerator overnight. Add the double cream to the cream cheese.

9. Add the Mango puree, Caster Sugar and Flour

- Add the Mango puree, sugar and flour to the cream cheese.

10. Blend Smoothly

- Use a hand mixer or a stand mixer to blend the ingredients together. Mix until the texture is smooth and all ingredients are well combined. Ensure there are no lumps.

11. Add the eggs

- Add the eggs, preferably one at a time, and scraping down the sides as you go, ensuring any unmixed ingredients are incorporated into the mix.

12. Pour onto the Base

- Once your cheesecake base has chilled, pour the cream cheese filling onto it, spreading it evenly, smoothing the top with a spoon.

13. Wrap and Bake

- Wrap the tin in silver foil, then clingfilm, then sliver foil, as per my suggestion in the Bain Marie section of this book.
- Bake at 170°C for an hour, or until golden brown on top but still wobbly in the centre.Once it reaches it's optimum state of being cooked, the cake should 'puff up' above the top of the tin, something that will drop as soon as you take the cake out of the oven. If you feel it requires longer, give it a little more time in the oven.

14. Cool and Chill

- After baking, open the oven door and allow the cheesecake to cool slightly. When ready, remove it from the oven and the Bain Marie, and allow it to cool to room temperature, preferably on a wire rack.
- Cover and refrigerate for at least eight hours, or preferably overnight before serving.

18. Preparing the topping

- Prepare the Gelatine by soaking the gelatine sheet in cold water according to package instructions until it becomes soft and pliable.

- Slice the three Passionfruit in half, and scoop out their innards into a bowl. Add 25g of Mango Purée and 30g of Caster Sugar to the mix.
- Heat the mixture over low-medium heat, stirring continuously until the sugar dissolves and the ingredients blend into a smooth consistency.
- Squeeze any excess water from the soaked gelatine sheet and add it to the mixture. Stir until the gelatine dissolves completely, contributing to the setting of the topping.
- Allow the topping mixture to cool slightly before pouring it over the baked and set cheesecake. This step ensures a smooth and even distribution of the topping.
- Place the cheesecake with the topping back into the refrigerator to allow it to set completely. This should only take an hour or so, before the cake is ready to serve.

13

WHITE CHOCOLATE & RASPBERRY

Delight in the harmonious blend of flavors with our White Chocolate Raspberry Cheesecake. Picture a classic cheesecake infused with the richness of White Belgian Chocolate, creating a velvety indulgence that forms the foundation of this delightful treat.

Crowning this creation is a homemade raspberry coulis, radiating with fruity freshness that complements the sweet notes of white chocolate. Each cake is then adorned with an abundance of raspberries, adding a burst of tartness and visual charm.

The result is a surprising and delightful experience that has become a favorite among our regular customers. Interestingly, it's also a temptation our staff members find hard to resist, indulging in this treat far too regularly. It's a testament to the irresistible allure of this White Chocolate Raspberry Cheesecake.

Base
  260g digestive biscuits
  90g unsalted butter
  10g caster sugar

Filling
   250g white chocolate
   900g Cream Cheese
   250ml double cream
   90g caster sugar
   30g plain flour
   I tsp Vanilla paste
   4 eggs

Topping
   1 gelatine strip
   Sauté 120g raspberries
   20g caster sugar
   12 raspberries for decoration

Instructions:

1. Prepare the Biscuits

- Place the digestive biscuits in a food processor.
- Pulse until the biscuits turn into fine crumbs.

2. Melt the Butter

- In a saucepan or microwave-safe bowl, melt the unsalted butter.

3. Combine Biscuits and Butter

- In the food processor, combine the biscuit crumbs with the caster sugar. Add the melted butter to this mixture.

4. Mix Thoroughly

- Blitz the ingredients together for a few seconds until the biscuit crumbs are evenly coated with the melted butter and sugar. The mixture should resemble damp sand.

5. Prepare the Tin

- Take a 9-inch springform tin, which should be sprayed and lined.
- Pour the biscuit mixture into the base of the tin, and spread it out evenly, using a fork. Use the back of a spoon or the bottom of a glass to compact the mixture. Keep the pressure light but firm.

6. Chill the Base

- Place the tin in the refrigerator and let the base chill for 20 minutes or so. This helps the butter solidify, creating a firm foundation for your cheesecake.

7. Preheat the Oven

- Preheat your oven to 170°C.

8. Melt the White Chocolate

- In a glass bowl, break the 250g of white chocolate into small chunks. Place the glass bowl over a pot of simmering water. Or, melt the chocolate in the microwave.

9. Prepare the Cream Cheese

- In a large mixing bowl, place the cream cheese. Ensure it's at room temperature for smoother blending. If at all possible, buy your cream cheese the day before baking, and leave it out of the refrigerator overnight. Add the double cream to the cream cheese.

10. Add the Caster Sugar, Vanilla and Flour

- Add the Caster Sugar, Vanilla Extract and Flour to the Cream Cheese.

11. Blend Smoothly

- Use a hand mixer or a stand mixer to blend the ingredients together. Mix until the texture is smooth and all ingredients are well combined. Ensure there are no lumps.

12. Add the eggs

- Add the eggs, preferably one at a time, and scraping down the sides as you go, ensuring any unmixed ingredients are incorporated into the mix.

13. Add the melted white chocolate

- As the last of the eggs blend into the mix, finally add the melted White Chocolate slowly into the batter, as you continue to beat the mixture into a smooth, velvety concoction.

14. Pour onto the Base

- Once your cheesecake base has chilled, pour the cream cheese filling onto it, spreading it evenly, smoothing the top with a spoon.

15. Wrap and Bake

- Wrap the tin in silver foil, then clingfilm, then sliver foil, as per my suggestion in the Bain Marie section of this book.
- Bake at 170ºC for an hour, or until somewhat brown on top but still wobbly in the centre.Once it reaches it's optimum state of being cooked, the cake should 'puff up' above the top of the tin, something that will drop as soon as you take the cake out of the oven. If you feel it requires longer, give it a little more time in the oven.

16. Cool and Chill

- After baking, open the oven door and allow the cheesecake to cool slightly. When ready, remove it from the oven and the Bain Marie, and allow it to cool to room temperature, preferably on a wire rack.
- Cover and refrigerate for at least eight hours, or preferably overnight before serving.

17. Preparing the topping

- Prepare the Gelatine by soaking the gelatine sheet in cold water according to package instructions until it becomes soft and pliable.

- Blitz the raspberries in a food processor and add 20g of Caster Sugar to the mix.
- Heat the mixture over low-medium heat, stirring continuously until the sugar dissolves and the ingredients blend into a smooth consistency.
- Squeeze any excess water from the soaked gelatine sheet and add it to the mixture. Stir until the gelatine dissolves completely, contributing to the setting of the topping.
- Allow the topping mixture to cool slightly before pouring it over the baked and set cheesecake. This step ensures a smooth and even distribution of the topping. Place 12 raspberries around the edges of the cake for decoration of each slice.
- Place the cheesecake with the topping back into the refrigerator to allow it to set completely. This should only take an hour or so, before the cake is ready to serve.

14

MATCHA

Embark on a culinary adventure with our Matcha Cheesecake – a uniquely green creation that sets itself apart from Pistachio or Avocado. Infused with the wonderfully fragrant Japanese green tea, this cheesecake harmoniously blends the essence of Matcha with our classic cheesecake mix.

This exotic creation is a wonderful thing to behold and savor with each decadent bite. Its gloriously green appearance is a testament to the captivating fusion of flavors within. Our Matcha Cheesecake invites you to experience a delightful journey into the realm of unique tastes, where the vibrancy of Matcha takes center stage in a truly indulgent treat.

Choosing a high-quality matcha powder is the key to unlocking a truly delightful culinary experience. The nuanced flavor profile, marked by a harmonious blend of sweetness, umami, and a subtle bitterness, elevates this cake to new heights. The vibrant green color not only enhances the visual appeal but also signifies the freshness and excellence of the tea leaves.

Base

260g digestive biscuits
90g unsalted butter
10g caster sugar

Filling
900g Cream Cheese
200ml double cream
160g caster sugar
4 tsp good quality matcha powder
20g plain flour
4 eggs

Instructions:

1. Prepare the Biscuits

- Place the digestive biscuits in a food processor.
- Pulse until the biscuits turn into fine crumbs.

2. Melt the Butter

- In a saucepan or microwave-safe bowl, melt the unsalted butter.

3. Combine Biscuits and Butter

- In the food processor, combine the biscuit crumbs with the caster sugar. Add the melted butter to this mixture.

4. Mix Thoroughly

- Blitz the ingredients together in the processor for a few seconds until the biscuit crumbs are evenly coated with the melted butter and sugar. The mixture should resemble damp sand.

5. Prepare the Tin

- Take a 9-inch springform tin, which should be sprayed and lined.
- Pour the biscuit mixture into the base of the tin, and spread it out evenly, using a fork. Use the back of a spoon or the bottom of a glass to compact the mixture. Keep the pressure light but firm.

6. Chill the Base

- Place the tin in the refrigerator and let the base chill for 20 minutes or so. This helps the butter solidify, creating a firm foundation for your cheesecake.

7. Preheat the Oven

- Preheat your oven to 170°C.

8. Prepare the Cream Cheese

- In a large mixing bowl, place the cream cheese. Ensure it's at room temperature for smoother blending. If at all possible, buy your cream cheese the day before baking, and leave it out of the refrigerator overnight. Add the double cream to the cream cheese.

9. Incorporate Sugar

- Sprinkle the caster sugar into the bowl with the cream cheese and condensed milk.

10. Add the Matcha Powder

- Add 4tsps of Matcha Powder to the mixture.

11. Sift in Flour

- Sift the plain flour into the bowl to avoid any lumps in the filling.

12. Blend Smoothly

- Use a hand mixer or a stand mixer to blend the ingredients together. Mix until the texture is smooth and all ingredients are well combined. Ensure there are no lumps.

13. Add the eggs

- Add the eggs, preferably one at a time, and scraping down the sides as you go, ensuring any unmixed ingredients are incorporated into the mix.

14. Pour onto the Base

- Once your cheesecake base has chilled, pour the cream cheese filling onto it, spreading it evenly, smoothing the top with a spoon.

15. Wrap and Bake

- Wrap the tin in silver foil, then clingfilm, then sliver foil, as per my suggestion in the Bain Marie section of this book.
- Bake at 170ºC for an hour, or until nicely cooked on top but still wobbly in the centre.Once it reaches it's optimum state of being cooked, the cake should 'puff up' above the top of the tin, something that will drop as soon as you take the cake out of the oven. If you feel it requires longer, give it a little more time in the oven.

16. Cool and Chill

- After baking, open the oven door and allow the cheesecake to cool slightly. When ready, remove it from the oven and the Bain Marie, and allow it to cool to room temperature, preferably on a wire rack.
- Cover and refrigerate for at least eight hours, or preferably overnight before serving.

If you have time, dip fresh strawberries in melting white chocolate, placing each one on a sheet of baking paper following dipping. Then, refrigerate them for an hour, before placing them on top of your gloriously green cheesecake! Totally optional, but it seemed to work nicely for us.

15

BLUEBERRY

The glorious purple creation! Envision the artistry unfolding as fabulous ripe blueberries entwine with the classic cheesecake mix, creating a mesmerizing marbling effect. Picture the crowning glory – a decadent blueberry glaze generously poured over the top, adding the perfect finishing touch to this indulgent delight.

As you gather your ingredients, the anticipation builds without the need for a detailed baking journey. Imagine the vibrant colors and rich aromas filling your kitchen, setting the stage for the creation of a culinary masterpiece.

Adding a poetic touch, let's revisit the timeless words of an old poem – "When I am old, I shall wear purple." Yet, in this modern twist, why not say, "eat purple" now? Each slice not only indulges your senses but also contributes to your 'five a day,' making the experience even sweeter.

Visualize the kitchen transforming into a haven of creativity, with the oven coaxing out the flavors and the blueberry dance within the cheesecake coming to life. The end result is not just a baked treat; it's a sweet symphony for your taste buds, an edible masterpiece that combines artistry with indulgence.

As you navigate the process without a detailed baking journey, relish the joy in each step. The Blueberry Marbled Cheesecake stands as a testament to your creative prowess, bringing a burst of color, flavor, and sheer delight to your kitchen.

Base

260g digestive biscuits

90g unsalted butter

10g caster sugar

Filling

900g Cream Cheese

250ml double cream

120g caster sugar

1tsp vanilla extract

50g plain flour

180g blueberries blitzed

4 eggs

Topping:

1/2 leaf gelatine

60g blueberries blitzed plus 1/2 lime

15g caster sugar

Handful of blueberries to decorate (optional)

Instructions:

1. Prepare the Biscuits

- Place the digestive biscuits in a food processor.

- Pulse until the biscuits turn into fine crumbs.

2. Melt the Butter

- In a saucepan or microwave-safe bowl, melt the unsalted butter.

3. Combine Biscuits and Butter

- In the food processor, combine the biscuit crumbs with the caster sugar. Add the melted butter to this mixture.

4. Mix Thoroughly

- Blitz the ingredients together in the food processor for a few seconds, until the biscuit crumbs are evenly coated with the melted butter and sugar. The mixture should resemble damp sand.

5. Prepare the Tin

- Take a 9-inch springform tin, which should be sprayed and lined.
- Pour the biscuit mixture into the base of the tin, and spread it out evenly, using a fork. Use the back of a spoon or the bottom of a glass to compact the mixture. Keep the pressure light but firm.

6. Chill the Base

- Place the tin in the refrigerator and let the base chill for 20 minutes or so. This helps the butter solidify, creating a firm foundation for your cheesecake.

7. Preheat the Oven

- Preheat your oven to 170°C.

8. Prepare the Cream Cheese

- In a large mixing bowl, place the cream cheese. Ensure it's at room temperature for smoother blending. If at all possible, buy your cream cheese the day before baking, and leave it out of the refrigerator overnight. Add the double cream to the cream cheese.

9. Incorporate Sugar

- Sprinkle the caster sugar into the bowl with the cream cheese.

10. Add the Vanilla Extract

- Add 1 tsp of Vanilla Extract to the mixture.

11. Sift in Flour

- Sift the 50g of plain flour into the bowl to avoid any lumps in the filling.

12. Blend Smoothly

- Use a hand mixer or a stand mixer to blend the ingredients together. Mix until the texture is smooth and all ingredients are well combined. Ensure there are no lumps.

13. Add the eggs

- Add the eggs, preferably one at a time, and scraping down the sides as you go, ensuring any unmixed ingredients are incorporated into the mix.

14. Blitz the Blueberries

- Briefly blitz the blueberries in a food processor so that they mainly turn to liquid, although you may want them to retain some of their shape.

15. Marble the Blueberries through the cake

- This is not remotely difficult. Essentially, pour the blitzed blueberries into the cheesecake batter in one go and, using a spatula, blend them together. You can either do this in a small way, creating a marbling effect, or you can mix them together until the entire cheesecake mix is purple. It's entirely up to you! It essentially tastes the same, so it's more an aesthetic thing.

16. Pour onto the Base

- Once your cheesecake base has chilled, pour the cream cheese filling onto it, spreading it evenly, smoothing the top with a spoon.

17. Wrap and Bake

- Wrap the tin in silver foil, then clingfilm, then sliver foil, as per my suggestion in the Bain Marie section of this book.
- Bake at 170°C for an hour, or until nicely cooked on top but still wobbly in the centre.Once it reaches it's optimum state of being cooked, the cake should 'puff up' above the top of the tin, something that will drop as soon as you take the cake out of the oven. If you feel it requires longer, give it a little more time in the oven.

19. Cool and Chill

- After baking, open the oven door and allow the cheesecake to cool slightly. When ready, remove it from the oven and the Bain Marie, and allow it to cool to room temperature, preferably on a wire rack.
- Cover and refrigerate for at least eight hours, or preferably overnight before serving.

19. Preparing the topping

- Prepare the Gelatine by soaking the gelatine sheet in cold water according to package instructions until it becomes soft and pliable.
- As before for the cake itself, briefly blitz the Blueberries in a food processor and add 15g of Caster Sugar to the mix, together with the juice of half a lime (optional).
- Heat the mixture over low–medium heat, stirring continuously until the sugar dissolves.
- Squeeze any excess water from the soaked gelatine sheet

and add it to the mixture. Stir until the gelatine dissolves completely, contributing to the setting of the topping.

· Allow the topping mixture to cool slightly before pouring it over the baked and set cheesecake. This step ensures a smooth and even distribution of the topping. Now, at this point, you can if you wish add even more blueberries to the top of the cheesecake. This is entirely up to you. Just be aware that more blueberries on top can make the cake harder to cut, but it does look very pretty.

· Place the cheesecake with the topping back into the refrigerator to allow it to set completely. This should only take an hour or so, before the cake is ready to serve.

16

CHOCOLATE

Embark on a journey of pure imagination and indulgence with this, our rather fab Chocolate Cheesecake, a divine fusion that seamlessly marries two beloved worlds. Envision the creation of this extraordinary treat – a luscious blend of rich dark chocolate intricately woven into our classic cheesecake mix. The result is a decadent symphony of flavors, carefully baked to absolute perfection.

As you anticipate the unveiling of this dark beauty, imagine the crowning touch – white-chocolate dipped strawberries artfully adorning the top. This visual and flavorful masterpiece adds an extra layer of sophistication, elevating the indulgence to new heights.

For those who insist that certain unions should not exist, the Chocolate Cheesecake is here to challenge such notions. One bite of this exquisite creation will redefine their expectations and celebrate the harmonious marriage of chocolate and cheesecake in every velvety mouthful. It's not just a dessert; it's a culinary revelation that proves some combinations are meant to be, delighting the palate with each rich and sumptuous bite.

So, let your imagination savor the luxurious blend of dark chocolate and classic cheesecake, and allow the velvety mouthfuls of our creation to transport you to a realm where indulgence knows no bounds. Whether you're a purist or an adventurous palate, this Chocolate Cheesecake promises an experience that transcends expectations, inviting you to revel in the sheer bliss of this divine fusion.

Base
    250g digestive biscuits
    90g unsalted butter
    10g caster sugar
    15g cocoa powder

Filling
    900g cream cheese
    250g double cream
    100g caster sugar
    100g light brown sugar
    20g plain flour
    200g dark cooking chocolate
    4 eggs

Instructions:

1.Prepare the Biscuits

- Place the digestive biscuits in a food processor and blitz them to fine crumbs.

2. Melt the Butter

- In a saucepan or microwave-safe bowl, melt the unsalted butter.

3. Combine Biscuits, Sugar, Cocoa Powder and Butter

- In the food processor combine the biscuit crumbs with the caster sugar and the cocoa powder, giving it a brief mix to ensure everything is combined. Add the melted butter to this mixture.

4. Mix Thoroughly

- Blitz the ingredients together for a few seconds in the food processor until the biscuit crumbs are evenly coated with the melted butter, cocoa powder and sugar. The mixture should resemble damp sand.

5. Prepare the Tin

- Take a 9-inch springform tin, which should be sprayed and lined.
- Pour the biscuit mixture into the base of the tin, and spread it out evenly, using a fork. Use the back of a spoon or the bottom of a glass to compact the mixture. Keep the pressure light but firm.

6. Chill the Base

- Place the tin in the refrigerator and let the base chill for 20 minutes or so. This helps the butter solidify, creating a firm foundation for your cheesecake.

7. Preheat the Oven

- Preheat your oven to 170ºC.

8. Melt the Dark Chocolate

- In a glass bowl, break the 200g of dark chocolate into small chunks. Place the glass bowl over a pot of simmering water. Or, melt the chocolate in the microwave.

9. Prepare the Cream Cheese

- In a large mixing bowl, place the cream cheese. Ensure it's at room temperature for smoother blending. If at all possible, buy your cream cheese the day before baking, and leave it out of the refrigerator overnight. Add the double cream to the cream cheese.

10. Add the Caster Sugar, LIght Brown Sugar and Flour

- Add the Caster Sugar, Light Brown Sugar and Flour to the Cream Cheese.

11. Blend Smoothly

- Use a hand mixer or a stand mixer to blend the ingredients together. Mix until the texture is smooth and all ingredients are well combined. Ensure there are no lumps.

12. Add the eggs

- Add the eggs, preferably one at a time, and scraping down the sides as you go, ensuring any unmixed ingredients are incorporated into the mix.

13. Add the melted dark chocolate to the cheesecake mix

- Because chocolate can be difficult to work with, this stage requires some care. Taking a large dessert spoon, add three spoonfuls of cream cheese mix to the melted chocolate in the bowl. Mix these together thoroughly by hand, before adding another three spoonfuls to the chocolate mix. Again, mix these together thoroughly by hand, and repeat this process until the entire cheesecake mix has been incorporated into the chocolate. I then usually pour everything back into the original cheesecake mixing bowl and give it one final blitz before pouring it out into the base.

14. Pour onto the Base

- Once your chocolate cheesecake base has chilled, pour the chocolate cream cheese filling onto it, spreading it evenly, smoothing the top with a spoon.

15. Wrap and Bake

- Wrap the tin in silver foil, then clingfilm, then sliver foil, as per my suggestion in the Bain Marie section of this book.
- Bake at 170°C for an hour, or until somewhat brown on top but still wobbly in the centre.Once it reaches it's optimum state of being cooked, the cake should 'puff up' above the top of the tin, something that will drop as soon as you take

the cake out of the oven. If you feel it requires longer, give it a little more time in the oven.

16. Cool and Chill

- After baking, open the oven door and allow the cheesecake to cool slightly. When ready, remove it from the oven and the Bain Marie, and allow it to cool to room temperature, preferably on a wire rack.
- Cover and refrigerate for at least eight hours, or preferably overnight before serving.

If you have time, dip fresh strawberries in melting white, dark, or milk chocolate, placing each one on a sheet of baking paper following dipping. Then, refrigerate them for an hour, before placing them on top of your fabulous chocolate creation! Totally optional, but it seemed to work nicely for us.

17

SNICKERS

Savor the unparalleled delight of one of the greatest combinations ever crafted – Chocolate and Peanut Butter – in our decadent creation.

Imagine the marriage of velvety peanut butter with our classic cheesecake mix, a symphony of flavors that culminates in a luscious, giant Snickers bar-inspired masterpiece.

Topped with a rich chocolate ganache, this indulgence is a year-round sensation for those who relish the divine alliance of nuts and chocolate. A definite crowd-pleaser, as long as there are no nut allergies in the mix, of course!

It is now possible to purchase mini sized Snickers in most supermarkets. These look really neat on top of the cake, so if you can get these, as opposed to chopping up larger Snickers bars, do so.

Base
    200g digestive biscuits
    50g salted peanuts, blitzed
    90g unsalted butter

10g caster sugar

15g cocoa powder

Filling

800g Cream Cheese

300g double cream

100g light brown sugar

100g caster sugar

3 spoons peanut butter (150g)

4 eggs

Topping

1/2 leaf gelatine

40g Nutella melted

50g double cream

3 Snickers bars for decoration

Instructions:

1.Prepare the Biscuits and the peanuts

- Blitz the peanuts first in the food processor. You can either blitz them until they are fine like small crumbs or, as I prefer, lightly blitz them so that they still retain some shape. Remove them from the food processor and set them aside for a moment.
- Place the digestive biscuits in a food processor and blitz them to fine crumbs.

2. Melt the Butter

- In a saucepan or microwave-safe bowl, melt the unsalted butter.

3. Combine Biscuits, Sugar, Peanuts, Cocoa Powder and Butter

- In the food processor bowl, combine the biscuit crumbs with the caster sugar and the blitzed peanuts, giving it a brief mix to ensure everything is combined. Add the melted butter to this mixture.

4. Mix Thoroughly

- Blitz the ingredients together for five seconds or so, until the biscuit crumbs are evenly coated with the melted butter, cocoa powder and sugar. The mixture should resemble damp sand.

5. Prepare the Tin

- Take a 9-inch springform tin, which should be sprayed and lined.
- Pour the biscuit mixture into the base of the tin, and spread it out evenly, using a fork. Use the back of a spoon or the bottom of a glass to compact the mixture. Keep the pressure light but firm.

6. Chill the Base

- Place the tin in the refrigerator and let the base chill for 20 minutes or so. This helps the butter solidify, creating a firm foundation for your cheesecake.

7. Preheat the Oven

- Preheat your oven to 170°C.

8. Prepare the Cream Cheese

- In a large mixing bowl, place the cream cheese. Ensure it's at room temperature for smoother blending. If at all possible, buy your cream cheese the day before baking, and leave it out of the refrigerator overnight. Add the double cream to the bowl.

9. Incorporate both sets of sugar

- Sprinkle the caster sugar and the light brown sugar into the bowl with the cream cheese.

10. Add the Peanut Butter

- Add 150g of Peanut Butter to the mix.

11. Blend Smoothly

- Use a hand mixer or a stand mixer to blend the ingredients together. Mix until the texture is smooth and all ingredients are well combined. Ensure there are no lumps.

12. Add the eggs

- Add the eggs, preferably one at a time, and scraping down the sides as you go, ensuring any unmixed ingredients are incorporated into the mix.

13. Pour onto the Base

- Once your cheesecake base has chilled, pour the peanut butter cream cheese filling onto it, spreading it evenly, smoothing the top with a spoon.

14. Wrap and Bake

- Wrap the tin in silver foil, then clingfilm, then sliver foil, as per my suggestion in the Bain Marie section of this book.
- Bake at 170°C for an hour, or until nicely cooked on top but still wobbly in the centre. Once it reaches it's optimum state of being cooked, the cake should 'puff up' above the top of the tin, something that will drop as soon as you take the cake out of the oven. If you feel it requires longer, give it a little more time in the oven.

15. Cool and Chill

- After baking, open the oven door and allow the cheesecake to cool slightly. When ready, remove it from the oven and the Bain Marie, and allow it to cool to room temperature, preferably on a wire rack.
- Cover and refrigerate for at least eight hours, or preferably overnight.

16. Preparing the topping

- Prepare the Gelatine by soaking the 1/2 gelatine sheet in cold water according to package instructions until it becomes soft and pliable.

- Spoon 40g of Nutella into a glass bowl.
- Heat the mixture over low-medium heat, stirring continuously until the Nutella melts. Once this happens, add the 50g of double cream and mix them together.
- Squeeze any excess water from the soaked gelatine sheet and add it to the mixture. Stir until the gelatine dissolves completely, contributing to the setting of the topping.
- As soon as it is ready, pour the mix over the baked and set cheesecake. Do not wait for it to cool! This step ensures a smooth and even distribution of the topping.
- Chop the three snickers bars into quarters, and place the resultant 12 mini slices of Snickers bars around the edges of the cakes, allowing the now-setting chocolate hazelnut topping to hold them in place.
- Place the cheesecake with the topping back into the refrigerator to allow it to set completely. This should only take an hour or so, before the cake is ready to serve.

18

CREME BRÛLÉE

Our Creme Brûlée Cheesecake blends the creamy richness of cheesecake and the caramelized sweetness of classic creme brûlée. Crafted on a buttery biscuit base, each bite harmonizes smooth vanilla custard with the subtle tang of cream cheese.

The result will be a delightful creation that captures the essence of both cheesecake and creme brûlée, satisfying your taste buds with every delectable slice.

Enjoy the process of bringing this harmonious dessert to life, and relish the delightful aroma that will fill your kitchen as it bakes to perfection.

Don't forget that you will need a chef's blowtorch to brown the top of the cake before serving. Don't, whatever you do, put the whole cake under your home grill! That works well for small crème brûlée desserts made in ramekins, but will cause an almighty mess if you attempt such a thing with a cheesecake in a springform tin.

Base

    260g digestive biscuits

90g unsalted butter
10g caster sugar

Filling
800g Cream Cheese
200ml double cream
1 tin condensed milk
30g caster sugar
2 tsp vanilla extract
25g plain flour
Yellow food colouring (optional)
4 eggs (preferably with very bright yokes)

Topping:
30g caster sugar

Equipment: chef's blowtorch

Instructions:

1. **Prepare the Biscuits**

- Place the digestive biscuits in a food processor.
- Pulse the biscuits into fine crumbs.

2. **Melt the Butter**

- In a saucepan or microwave-safe bowl, melt the unsalted butter.

3. **Combine Biscuits and Butter**

- In the food processor, combine the biscuit crumbs with the caster sugar. Add the melted butter to this mixture.

4. Mix Thoroughly

- Blitz the ingredients together for a few seconds until the biscuit crumbs are evenly coated with the melted butter and sugar. The mixture should resemble damp sand.

5. Prepare the Tin

- Take a 9-inch springform tin, which should be sprayed and lined.
- Pour the biscuit mixture into the base of the tin, and spread it out evenly, using a fork. Use the back of a spoon or the bottom of a glass to compact the mixture. Keep the pressure light but firm.

6. Chill the Base

- Place the tin in the refrigerator and let the base chill for 20 minutes or so. This helps the butter solidify, creating a firm foundation for your cheesecake.

7. Preheat the Oven

- Preheat your oven to 170°C.

8. Prepare the Cream Cheese

- In a large mixing bowl, place the cream cheese. Ensure it's at

room temperature for smoother blending. If at all possible, buy your cream cheese the day before baking, and leave it out of the refrigerator overnight. Add the double cream.

9. Add the Condensed Milk

- Open the tin of condensed milk and add it to the cream cheese and double cream.

10. Incorporate Sugar

- Sprinkle the caster sugar into the bowl with the cream cheese and condensed milk.

11. Add Vanilla Paste, Vanilla Extract and Yellow Food Colouring

- Add the 2 teaspoons of vanilla extract and, if you wish, a teaspoon of Yellow Food Colouring to the mixture.

12. Sift in Flour

- Sift the plain flour into the bowl to avoid any lumps in the filling.

13. Blend Smoothly

- Use a hand mixer or a stand mixer to blend the ingredients together. Mix until the texture is smooth and all ingredients are well combined. Ensure there are no lumps.

14. Add the eggs

- Add the eggs, preferably one at a time, and scraping down the sides as you go, ensuring any unmixed ingredients are incorporated into the mix.

15. Pour onto the Base

- Once your cheesecake base has chilled, pour the cream cheese filling onto it, spreading it evenly, smoothing the top with a spoon.

16. Wrap and Bake

- Wrap the tin in silver foil, then clingfilm, then sliver foil, as per my suggestion in the Bain Marie section of this book.
- Bake at 170°C for an hour, or until golden brown on top but still wobbly in the centre. Once it reaches it's optimum state of being cooked, the cake should 'puff up' above the top of the tin, something that will drop as soon as you take the cake out of the oven. If you feel it requires longer, give it a little more time in the oven.

17. Cool and Chill

- After baking, open the oven door and allow the cheesecake to cool slightly. When ready, remove it from the oven and the Bain Marie, and allow it to cool to room temperature, preferably on a wire rack.
- Cover and refrigerate for at least eight hours, or preferably overnight.

18. Topping

- Once the cheesecake has completely set, and just before serving, remove it from the fridge and sprinkle approximately 30g of caster sugar over the surface. Ensure the sugar is spread evenly to cover the entire surface.
- Use a kitchen torch to melt and caramelize the sugar. Hold the flame a few inches away and move it in a circular motion until the sugar turns golden brown and forms a crispy crust.
- Allow the caramelized sugar to cool and harden for a minute or two before serving.
- Remember to keep a watchful eye while caramelizing to prevent burning. This quick and easy process adds a delightful crunchy layer, transforming your Creme Brûlée into a delectable treat.

19

BANOFFEE

The Banoffee Cheesecake was a rather late addition to our menu. In crafting this delightful treat, we took the ripest bananas, and smashed them together with a heavenly blend of caramel and cream, all nestled on a buttery biscuit base. Each bite promises a symphony of flavors that dance on your taste buds.

Fun fact: The Banoffee pie, from which this cheesecake draws inspiration, has an interesting origin. Nigel Mackenzie and Ian Dowding, owner and chef of the former Hungry Monk Restaurant in Jevington, East Sussex, claim to have pioneered the dessert back in the 1970s. Their creation was inspired by a San Francisco recipe for "Blum's Coffee Toffee Pie."

Once you've made this cake, it's a good idea to whip up a large batch of whipped cream, which you then can serve on the side of each slice. Your guests can then add as much or as little as they like to their dessert. It's a very rich cheesecake this one, so if they overdo it, they'll only have themselves to blame!

Base

260g digestive biscuits
90g unsalted butter
10g caster sugar

Filling:
900g Cream Cheese
250ml double cream
3 large ripe bananas, blitzed in the food processor (creating about 150g of pulp
120g caster sugar
30g plain flour
4 eggs

For the toffee swirl:
50g caramel
100g dark brown sugar
50ml cream swirled through

Topping
1/2 gelatine sheet.
50g dark brown sugar
50ml double cream
50g caramel
Double Cream whipped (optional)
Chocolate shavings (optional)

Instructions:

1. Prepare the Biscuits

- Place the digestive biscuits in a food processor.

- Pulse the biscuits into fine crumbs.

2. Melt the Butter

- In a saucepan or microwave-safe bowl, melt the unsalted butter.

3. Combine Biscuits and Butter

- In the food processor, combine the biscuit crumbs with the caster sugar. Add the melted butter to this mixture.

4. Mix Thoroughly

- Blitz the ingredients together for a few seconds until the biscuit crumbs are evenly coated with the melted butter and sugar. The mixture should resemble damp sand.

5. Prepare the Tin

- Take a 9-inch springform tin, which should be sprayed and lined.
- Pour the biscuit mixture into the base of the tin, and spread it out evenly, using a fork. Use the back of a spoon or the bottom of a glass to compact the mixture. Keep the pressure light but firm.

6. Chill the Base

- Place the tin in the refrigerator and let the base chill for 20 minutes or so. This helps the butter solidify, creating a firm foundation for your cheesecake.

7. Preheat the Oven

- Preheat your oven to 170°C.

8. Prepare the Cream Cheese

- In a large mixing bowl, place the cream cheese. Ensure it's at room temperature for smoother blending. If at all possible, buy your cream cheese the day before baking, and leave it out of the refrigerator overnight. Add the double cream to the cream cheese.

9. Add the bananas

- Having blitzed the three ripe bananas in your food processor, add them to the cream cheese.

10. Incorporate Sugar

- Sprinkle the caster sugar into the bowl with the cream cheese and smashed banana.

11. Sift in Flour

- Sift the plain flour into the bowl to avoid any lumps in the filling.

12. Blend Smoothly

- Use a hand mixer or a stand mixer to blend the ingredients together. Mix until the texture is smooth and all ingredients are well combined. Ensure there are no lumps.

13. Add the eggs

- Add the eggs, preferably one at a time, and scraping down the sides as you go, ensuring any unmixed ingredients are incorporated into the mix.

14. Make the toffee sauce

- Over a pan of simmering water, in a separate bowl, melt and mix together the caramel, dark brown sugar, and 50ml of double cream. Once the caramel has melted and the dark brown sugar has mixed in thoroughly, pour this into the cheesecake batter and fold it gently into the mix, creating a marbling effect.

15. Pour onto the Base

- Once your cheesecake base has chilled, pour the cheesecake filling onto it, spreading it evenly, smoothing the top with a spoon.

16. Wrap and Bake

- Wrap the tin in silver foil, then clingfilm, then sliver foil, as per my suggestion in the Bain Marie section of this book.
- Bake at 170°C for an hour, or until golden brown on top but still wobbly in the centre. Once it reaches it's optimum state

of being cooked, the cake should 'puff up' above the top of the tin, something that will drop as soon as you take the cake out of the oven. If you feel it requires longer, give it a little more time in the oven.

· The bananas are quite wet, so it may well require a little more time.

17. Cool and Chill

· After baking, open the oven door and allow the cheesecake to cool slightly. When ready, remove it from the oven and the Bain Marie, and allow it to cool to room temperature, preferably on a wire rack.

· Cover and refrigerate for at least eight hours, or preferably overnight.

18. Preparing the topping

· Prepare the Gelatine by soaking the gelatine sheet in cold water according to package instructions until it becomes soft and pliable.

· In a saucepan, mix together the dark brown sugar, the double cream, and caramel. Heat the mixture over low-medium heat, stirring continuously until the sugar dissolves and the ingredients blend into a smooth consistency.

· Squeeze any excess water from the soaked gelatine sheet and add it to the mixture. Stir until the gelatine dissolves completely, contributing to the setting of the topping.

· As soon as it is ready, pour it over the baked and set cheesecake. Place the cheesecake with the topping back into the refrigerator to allow it to set completely. This should only take an hour or so, before the cake is ready to serve.

You can serve with whipped cream and chocolate shavings. I have used both dark chocolate and salted caramel chocolate for this, and both work well.

20

BAILEYS

Here's a suggestion for Christmas! As you prepare to ring in the holiday season, consider the exquisite addition of a Baileys cheesecake to your festive table.

Picture the moment when your fork glides through the velvety layers of Baileys-infused filling, nestled atop a decadent buttery digestive biscuit crust. The rich and warming notes of Irish cream, coupled with the comforting crunch of the biscuit base, create a symphony of flavors that embodies the spirit of Christmas indulgence.

This seasonal treat isn't just a dessert; it's a centerpiece that invites loved ones to gather and savor the magic of the holidays together. As you slice through the creamy perfection and share a piece with family and friends, you're not just serving a cheesecake; you're crafting a cherished moment that encapsulates the joy, warmth, and togetherness of the festive season.

Serve with single pouring cream, or if you really don't have to do anything for the next few days, Brandy Cream.

Base

   260g digestive biscuits

   90g unsalted butter

   10g caster sugar

Filling

   900g Cream Cheese

   250ml double cream

   4 tbsps Baileys liquor

   100g caster sugar

   100g light brown sugar

   35g flour

   1 tsp Vanilla extract

   4 eggs

Instructions:

1. Prepare the Biscuits

- Place the digestive biscuits in a food processor.
- Pulse the biscuits into fine crumbs.

2. Melt the Butter

- In a saucepan or microwave-safe bowl, melt the unsalted butter.

3. Combine Biscuits and Butter

- In the food processor, combine the biscuit crumbs with the caster sugar. Add the melted butter to this mixture.

4. Mix Thoroughly

- Blitz the ingredients together for a few seconds until the biscuit crumbs are evenly coated with the melted butter and sugar. The mixture should resemble damp sand.

5. Prepare the Tin

- Take a 9-inch springform tin, which should be sprayed and lined.
- Pour the biscuit mixture into the base of the tin, and spread it out evenly, using a fork. Use the back of a spoon or the bottom of a glass to compact the mixture. Keep the pressure light but firm.

6. Chill the Base

- Place the tin in the refrigerator and let the base chill for 20 minutes or so. This helps the butter solidify, creating a firm foundation for your cheesecake.

7. Preheat the Oven

- Preheat your oven to 170°C.

8. Prepare the Cream Cheese

- In a large mixing bowl, place the cream cheese. Ensure it's at room temperature for smoother blending. If at all possible, buy your cream cheese the day before baking, and leave it out of the refrigerator overnight. Add the 250ml of double cream.

9. Add the Baileys

- Add 4 tablespoons of Baileys to the mix and don't worry too much about getting these amounts perfect! A little more never hurt anyone.

10. Incorporate Sugar

- Add both the caster sugar and the light brown sugar into the bowl with the cream cheese and Baileys.

11. Sift in Flour

- Sift the plain flour into the bowl to avoid any lumps in the filling.

12. Add Vanilla Extract

- Add one teaspoon of Vanilla Extract to the mix.

13. Blend Smoothly

- Use a hand mixer or a stand mixer to blend the ingredients together. Mix until the texture is smooth and all ingredients are well combined. Ensure there are no lumps.

14. Add the eggs

- Add the eggs, preferably one at a time, and scraping down

the sides as you go, ensuring any unmixed ingredients are incorporated into the mix.

15. Pour onto the Base

- Once your cheesecake base has chilled, pour the cheesecake filling onto it, spreading it evenly, smoothing the top with a spoon.

16. Wrap and Bake

- Wrap the tin in silver foil, then clingfilm, then sliver foil, as per my suggestion in the Bain Marie section of this book.
- Bake at 170°C for an hour, or until golden brown on top but still wobbly in the centre. Once it reaches it's optimum state of being cooked, the cake should 'puff up' above the top of the tin, something that will drop as soon as you take the cake out of the oven. If you feel it requires longer, give it a little more time in the oven.

17. Cool and Chill

- After baking, open the oven door and allow the cheesecake to cool slightly. When ready, remove it from the oven and the Bain Marie, and allow it to cool to room temperature, preferably on a wire rack.
- Cover and refrigerate for at least eight hours, or preferably overnight. Serve with single pouring cream.

BAILEYS
almand
DAIRY FREE
ALMOND DRINK

21

STRAWBERRY

Picture a strawberry cheesecake that's a symphony of flavors, with a luscious filling featuring the richness of cream and the warmth of vanilla.

Nestled on a buttery biscuit crust, this dessert becomes a delightful medley of textures and tastes. Ripe strawberries provide bursts of sweetness, harmonizing perfectly with the velvety cheesecake base. Each slice is a celebration of the classic combination of cream and vanilla, accentuated by the vibrant notes of fresh strawberries.

Whether enjoyed as a sweet ending to a meal or as a centerpiece for a special occasion, this strawberry cheesecake promises a decadent and satisfying experience for dessert enthusiasts.

I have also tried this in the past with ginger biscuits in the base, although they do have a habit of falling apart. I suspect the way around this is to do half digestive/half ginger biscuits. As always, never be afraid to experiment.

Base

260g digestive biscuits
90g unsalted butter
10g caster sugar

Filling
800g Cream Cheese
250ml double cream
1 tin condensed milk
40g caster sugar
I tsp Vanilla paste
25g plain flour
4 eggs

Topping:
Sauté 300g strawberries
15g sugar
1 gelatine leaf

Instructions:

1. Prepare the Biscuits

- Place the digestive biscuits in a food processor.
- Pulse the biscuits into fine crumbs.

2. Melt the Butter

- In a saucepan or microwave-safe bowl, melt the unsalted butter.

3. Combine Biscuits and Butter

- In the food processor, combine the biscuit crumbs with the caster sugar. Add the melted butter to this mixture.

4. Mix Thoroughly

- Blitz the ingredients together for a few seconds until the biscuit crumbs are evenly coated with the melted butter and sugar. The mixture should resemble damp sand.

5. Prepare the Tin

- Take a 9-inch springform tin, which should be sprayed and lined.
- Pour the biscuit mixture into the base of the tin, and spread it out evenly, using a fork. Use the back of a spoon or the bottom of a glass to compact the mixture. Keep the pressure light but firm.

6. Chill the Base

- Place the tin in the refrigerator and let the base chill for 20 minutes or so. This helps the butter solidify, creating a firm foundation for your cheesecake.

7. Preheat the Oven

- Preheat your oven to 160°C.

8. Prepare the Cream Cheese

- In a large mixing bowl, place the cream cheese. Ensure it's at

room temperature for smoother blending. If at all possible, buy your cream cheese the day before baking, and leave it out of the refrigerator overnight. Add the double cream.

9. Add the Condensed Milk

- Open the tin of condensed milk and add it to the cream cheese.

10. Incorporate Sugar

- Sprinkle the caster sugar into the bowl with the cream cheese and condensed milk.

11. Add Vanilla Paste

- Add the teaspoon of vanilla paste to the mixture.

12. Sift in Flour

- Sift the plain flour into the bowl to avoid any lumps in the filling.

13. Blend Smoothly

- Use a hand mixer or a stand mixer to blend the ingredients together. Mix until the texture is smooth and all ingredients are well combined. Ensure there are no lumps.

14. Add the eggs

- Add the eggs, preferably one at a time, and scraping down the sides as you go, ensuring any unmixed ingredients are incorporated into the mix.

15. Pour onto the Base

- Once your cheesecake base has chilled, pour the cream cheese filling onto it, spreading it evenly, smoothing the top with a spoon.

16. Wrap and Bake

- Wrap the tin in silver foil, then clingfilm, then sliver foil, as per my suggestion in the Bain Marie section of this book.
- Bake at 160°C for an hour, or until golden brown on top but still wobbly in the centre. Once it reaches it's optimum state of being cooked, the cake should 'puff up' above the top of the tin, something that will drop as soon as you take the cake out of the oven. If you feel it requires longer, give it a little more time in the oven.

17. Cool and Chill

- After baking, open the oven door and allow the cheesecake to cool slightly. When ready, remove it from the oven and the Bain Marie, and allow it to cool to room temperature, preferably on a wire rack.
- Cover and refrigerate for at least eight hours, or preferably overnight.

18. Preparing the topping

- Prepare the Gelatine by soaking the gelatine sheet in cold water according to package instructions until it becomes soft and pliable.
- If present, remove the leafy hull from your strawberries, so that only the red fruit remains. If your strawberries are particularly large, slice them in half.
- Place the strawberries in a frying pan or saucepan and add a tablespoon of water and 15g of caster sugar.
- Heat the fruit over a low-medium heat, stirring continuously until the sugar dissolves, the fruit is warm, and there is now some liquid to play with at the bottom of the pan. The strawberries will lose their colour a little, and some shape, so don't cook them for too long.
- Squeeze any excess water from the soaked gelatine sheet and add it to the mixture. Stir until the gelatine dissolves completely.
- Remove from the heat and using a spoon, cover each strawberry with some of the liquid, ensuring that the gelatine has, without doubt, covered each of the soft fruits.
- Allow the topping mixture to cool slightly before pouring it over the baked and set cheesecake. This step ensures a smooth and even distribution of the topping.
- Place the cheesecake with the topping back into the refrigerator to allow it to set completely. This should take approximately three hours, before the cake is ready to serve.

22

KINDER

Originally crafted by us for an Arabian prince's birthday, this Kinder Bueno cheesecake is a masterpiece of indulgence and sophistication.

Picture a luxurious chocolate biscuit crust laying the foundation for the decadent journey that follows. The creamy cheesecake filling, infused with the regal essence of Kinder Bueno, creates a symphony of flavors fit for royalty. Every slice is a testament to the creative process behind its inception – a dessert born from passion, precision, and a desire to elevate the celebration of a special occasion.

This Kinder Bueno cheesecake, with its rich chocolate biscuit crust, stands as a delectable embodiment of both opulence and homemade delight.

Base
  250g digestive biscuits
  90g unsalted butter
  10g caster sugar
  15g cocoa powder

Filling
   750g Cream Cheese
   150ml double cream
   1 tin condensed milk
   40g light brown soft sugar
   1 tsp Vanilla extract
   30g plain flour
   200g Nutella (melted)
   4 eggs

Topping:
   40g Nutella
   50g Double Cream
   ½ gelatine sheet
   3 Kinder Bars, each one divided into quarters, for decoration

Instructions:

1.Prepare the Biscuits

  · Place the digestive biscuits in a food processor and blitz
    them to fine crumbs.

2. Melt the Butter

  · In a saucepan or microwave-safe bowl, melt the unsalted
    butter.

3. Combine Biscuits, Sugar, Cocoa Powder and Butter

  · In the food processor combine the biscuit crumbs with the

caster sugar and the cocoa powder, giving it a brief mix to ensure everything is combined. Add the melted butter to this mixture.

4. Mix Thoroughly

· Blitz the ingredients together for a few seconds in the food processor until the biscuit crumbs are evenly coated with the melted butter, cocoa powder and sugar. The mixture should resemble damp sand.

5. Prepare the Tin

· Take a 9-inch springform tin, which should be sprayed and lined.
· Pour the biscuit mixture into the base of the tin, and spread it out evenly, using a fork. Use the back of a spoon or the bottom of a glass to compact the mixture. Keep the pressure light but firm.

6. Chill the Base

· Place the tin in the refrigerator and let the base chill for 20 minutes or so. This helps the butter solidify, creating a firm foundation for your cheesecake.

7. Preheat the Oven

· Preheat your oven to 160°C.

8. Melt the Nutella

- Melt 200g of Nutella in a glass bowl over a saucepan of simmering water. Continue to make the rest of the cake as this melts.

9. Prepare the Cream Cheese

- In a large mixing bowl, place the cream cheese. Ensure it's at room temperature for smoother blending. If at all possible, buy your cream cheese the day before baking, and leave it out of the refrigerator overnight. Add the double cream to the cream cheese.

10. Add the Condensed Milk

- Open the tin of condensed milk and add it to the cream cheese.

11. Incorporate Sugar

- Sprinkle the soft light brown sugar into the bowl with the cream cheese and condensed milk.

12. Add Vanilla Extract

- Add the teaspoon of vanilla extract to the mixture.

13. Sift in Flour

- Sift the plain flour into the bowl to avoid any lumps in the filling.

14. Blend Smoothly

- Use a hand mixer or a stand mixer to blend the ingredients together. Mix until the texture is smooth and all ingredients are well combined. Ensure there are no lumps.

15. Add the eggs

- Add the eggs, preferably one at a time, and scraping down the sides as you go, ensuring any unmixed ingredients are incorporated into the mix.

16. Fold in the melted Nutella

- Remove the bowl of melted Nutella from the heat. Pour into the cheesecake mix and, using a spatula, fold the melted chocolate into the batter. For a wonderful marbling effect, limit the number of times you fold the Nutella. Or, if you prefer a more chocolatey look, blend it in entirely. It's up to you, but it doesn't really make any difference to the overall taste and quality.

17. Pour onto the Base

- Once your chocolate cheesecake base has chilled, pour the cream cheese filling onto it, spreading it evenly, smoothing the top with a spoon.

18. Wrap and Bake

- Wrap the tin in silver foil, then clingfilm, then sliver foil, as per my suggestion in the Bain Marie section of this book.

- Bake at 160°C for an hour, or until golden brown on top but still wobbly in the centre. Once it reaches it's optimum state of being cooked, the cake should 'puff up' above the top of the tin, something that will drop as soon as you take the cake out of the oven. If you feel it requires longer, give it a little more time in the oven.

19. Cool and Chill

- After baking, open the oven door and allow the cheesecake to cool slightly. When ready, remove it from the oven and the Bain Marie, and allow it to cool to room temperature, preferably on a wire rack.
- Cover and refrigerate for at least eight hours, or preferably overnight before preparing the topping.

20. Preparing the topping

- Prepare the Gelatine by soaking the 1/2 gelatine sheet in cold water according to package instructions until it becomes soft and pliable.
- Spoon 40g of Nutella into a glass bowl.
- Heat the mixture over low-medium heat, stirring continuously until the Nutella melts. Once this happens, add the 50g of double cream and mix them together.
- Squeeze any excess water from the soaked gelatine sheet and add it to the mixture. Stir until the gelatine dissolves completely, contributing to the setting of the topping.
- As soon as it is ready, pour the mix over the baked and set cheesecake. Do not wait for it to cool! This step ensures a

smooth and even distribution of the topping.
- Chop the three Kinder Bueno bars into quarters, and place the resultant 12 mini slices of Kinder bars around the edges of the cakes, allowing the now-setting chocolate hazelnut topping to hold them in place.
- Place the cheesecake with the topping back into the refrigerator to allow it to set completely. This should only take an hour or so, before the cake is ready to serve.

23

LEMON

Immerse yourself in the vibrant flavors of our Lemon Cheese-cake, a true delight for the citrus enthusiast.

Picture a velvety cheesecake filling, expertly infused with the essence of zesty lemons, all set atop a buttery biscuit base. For those seeking a lighter and more traditional touch, revel in the balance of creamy texture and lively lemon flavor. For an optional twist, consider adding a luscious lemon curd topping at the end, enhancing the experience with a burst of tangy sweetness. I personally prefer the lemon curd topping for that extra citric kick.

This Lemon Cheesecake, with its refreshing profile and customizable touch, is an ideal choice to brighten up any occasion or satisfy your craving for a citrus-infused treat. This is another cheesecake whereby you could actually substitute a ginger biscuit base for the digestive base; but be aware that ginger biscuits on their own can fall apart, so a ginger/digestive mix might work better.

Base

260g digestive biscuits
90g unsalted butter
10g caster sugar
1 tbsp lemon curd

Filling
800g Cream Cheese
250ml double cream
1 tin condensed milk
2 lemons zest & juice
30g plain flour
4 eggs

Optional topping
100g lemon curd
1/3 gelatine leaf

Instructions:

1. Prepare the Biscuits

- Place the digestive biscuits in a food processor.
- Pulse the biscuits into fine crumbs.

2. Melt the Butter

- In a saucepan or microwave-safe bowl, melt the unsalted butter.

3. Combine Biscuits and Butter

- In the food processor, combine the biscuit crumbs with the caster sugar. Add the melted butter to this mixture.

4. Mix Thoroughly

- Blitz the ingredients together for a few seconds until the biscuit crumbs are evenly coated with the melted butter and sugar. The mixture should resemble damp sand.

5. Prepare the Tin

- Take a 9-inch springform tin, which should be sprayed and lined.
- Pour the biscuit mixture into the base of the tin, and spread it out evenly, using a fork. Use the back of a spoon or the bottom of a glass to compact the mixture. Keep the pressure light but firm.

6. Chill the Base

- Place the tin in the refrigerator and let the base chill for 20 minutes or so. This helps the butter solidify, creating a firm foundation for your cheesecake. Once it has set, remove the tin from the fridge, and slather approximately 1 tablespoon of lemon curd over the base, ensuring a well covered, yet thin coating. Return the tin to the fridge.

7. Preheat the Oven

- Preheat your oven to 160°C.

8. Prepare the Cream Cheese

- In a large mixing bowl, place the cream cheese. Ensure it's at room temperature for smoother blending. If at all possible, buy your cream cheese the day before baking, and leave it out of the refrigerator overnight. Add the double cream to the cream cheese.

9. Add the Condensed Milk

- Open the tin of condensed milk and add it to the cream cheese.

10. Add Lemon Zest and Juice

- Using a grater, finely zest the outside of 2 lemons into the cream cheese mix. Slice both lemons in half. Then, using a lemon squeezer, squeeze the juice of all four of the lemon halves into the cheesecake mix.

11. Sift in Flour

- Sift the plain flour into the bowl to avoid any lumps in the filling.

12. Blend Smoothly

- Use a hand mixer or a stand mixer to blend the ingredients together. Mix until the texture is smooth and all ingredients are well combined. Ensure there are no lumps.

13. Add the eggs

- Add the eggs, preferably one at a time, and scraping down the sides as you go, ensuring any unmixed ingredients are incorporated into the mix.

14. Pour onto the Base

- Once your cheesecake base has chilled and the lemon curd has set a little, pour the cream cheese filling onto it, spreading it evenly, smoothing the top with a spoon.

15. Wrap and Bake

- Wrap the tin in silver foil, then clingfilm, then sliver foil, as per my suggestion in the Bain Marie section of this book.
- Bake at 160°C for an hour, or until golden brown on top but still wobbly in the centre. Once it reaches it's optimum state of being cooked, the cake should 'puff up' above the top of the tin, something that will drop as soon as you take the cake out of the oven. If you feel it requires longer, give it a little more time in the oven.

16. Cool and Chill

- After baking, open the oven door and allow the cheesecake to cool slightly. When ready, remove it from the oven and the Bain Marie, and allow it to cool to room temperature, preferably on a wire rack.
- Cover and refrigerate for at least eight hours, or preferably overnight before making the topping.

17. Preparing the topping

- Prepare the small amount of gelatine by soaking the the sheet in cold water according to package instructions until it becomes soft and pliable.
- Heat the lemon curd in a glass bowl over a gently simmering pot of water. Allow it to gently melt.
- Squeeze any excess water from the soaked gelatine sheet and add it to the mixture. Stir until the gelatine dissolves completely.
- Pour the topping immediately over the baked and set cheese-cake. This step ensures a smooth and even distribution of the topping.
- Place the cheesecake with the topping back into the re-frigerator to allow it to set completely. This should take approximately half an hour, before the cake is ready to serve.

Serve with whipped double cream.

24

LOTUS BISCOFF

Savour the delightful Lotus Biscoff Cheesecake – a creamy sensation with a biscuit base, highlighted by the caramelized sweetness of Lotus Biscoff.

The subtle touch of cinnamon adds warmth, creating a timeless indulgence for those who relish the harmony of creamy texture and the distinct sweetness of Lotus Biscoff.

Although a late addition to our menu, this cheesecake quickly became a market favorite, selling out upon its debut. A testament to its irresistible blend of flavors that captivates dessert enthusiasts.

Base
   200g digestive biscuits
   60g Lotus Biscoff biscuits
   90g unsalted butter
   10g caster sugar

Filling
   900g Cream Cheese

250ml double cream
100g Lotus Biscoff paste
100g light brown sugar
100g caster sugar
1 tsp vanilla extract
20g plain flour
100g Lotus Biscuit crumbs on top

Instructions:

1. Prepare the Biscuits

- Place the digestive biscuits and Lotus Biscoff biscuits in a food processor.
- Pulse the biscuits into fine crumbs.

2. Melt the Butter

- In a saucepan or microwave-safe bowl, melt the unsalted butter.

3. Combine Biscuits and Butter

- In the food processor, combine the biscuit crumbs with the caster sugar. Add the melted butter to this mixture.

4. Mix Thoroughly

- Blitz the ingredients together for a few seconds until the biscuit crumbs are evenly coated with the melted butter and sugar. The mixture should resemble damp sand.

5. Prepare the Tin

- Take a 9-inch springform tin, which should be sprayed and lined.
- Pour the biscuit mixture into the base of the tin, and spread it out evenly, using a fork. Use the back of a spoon or the bottom of a glass to compact the mixture. Keep the pressure light but firm.

6. Chill the Base

- Place the tin in the refrigerator and let the base chill for 20 minutes or so. This helps the butter solidify, creating a firm foundation for your cheesecake.

7. Preheat the Oven

- Preheat your oven to 170°C.

8. Prepare the Cream Cheese

- In a large mixing bowl, place the cream cheese. Ensure it's at room temperature for smoother blending. If at all possible, buy your cream cheese the day before baking, and leave it out of the refrigerator overnight. Add the double cream to the cream cheese.

9. Add the Lotus Biscoff paste

- Add 100g of Lotus Biscoff paste to the cream cheese.

10. Incorporate Sugar

- Sprinkle the caster sugar and the light brown sugar into the bowl with the cream cheese and Lotus paste.

11. Add Vanilla Extract

- Add a teaspoon of Vanilla Extract to the mixture.

12. Sift in Flour

- Sift the plain flour into the bowl to avoid any lumps in the filling.

13. Blend Smoothly

- Use a hand mixer or a stand mixer to blend the ingredients together. Mix until the texture is smooth and all ingredients are well combined. Ensure there are no lumps.

14. Add the eggs

- Add the eggs, preferably one at a time, and scraping down the sides as you go, ensuring any unmixed ingredients are incorporated into the mix.

15. Pour onto the Base

- Once your cheesecake base has chilled, pour the cream cheese filling onto it, spreading it evenly, smoothing the top with a spoon.

16. Add Lotus Biscoff crumbs on top

- Blitz 100g of Lotus Biscoff biscuits in the food processor. You can grind them until they are completely smooth, or until they are small but coarse. Then, using a tablespoon, sprinkle them over the top of the cheesecake, pressing down lightly, so that the biscuit crumbs stick to the top of the cake. Do this untll the entire top of the cake is covered in biscuit crumb.

17. Wrap and Bake

- Wrap the tin in silver foil, then clingfilm, then sliver foil, as per my suggestion in the Bain Marie section of this book.
- Bake at 150°C for an hour and twenty minutes, or until golden brown on top but still wobbly in the centre. Once it reaches it's optimum state of being cooked, the cake should 'puff up' above the top of the tin, something that will drop as soon as you take the cake out of the oven.
- If you feel it requires longer, give it a little more time in the oven, as the biscuit topping will make this cake take longer to cook.

18. Cool and Chill

- After baking, open the oven door and allow the cheesecake to cool slightly. When ready, remove it from the oven and the Bain Marie, and allow it to cool to room temperature, preferably on a wire rack.
- Cover and refrigerate for at least eight hours, or preferably overnight.

Serve with Lotus Biscoff biscuits broken in half and placed around the plate and single cream or vanilla ice-cream.

25

CHOCOLATE ORANGE

Elevate your Easter and Christmas celebrations with our Chocolate Orange Cheesecake, a dessert that embodies the spirit of joy and indulgence.

Picture a velvety cheesecake, where the richness of chocolate meets the vibrant essence of orange, all set on a decadent chocolate biscuit base. The harmonious fusion of festive flavors creates a delightful treat, making it the perfect addition to your holiday gatherings.

Whether served as a centerpiece or enjoyed as a sweet finale, this Chocolate Orange Cheesecake promises to be a festive favorite, spreading warmth and delight during the holiday season.

Base
  250g digestive biscuits
  90g unsalted butter
  10g caster sugar
  15g cocoa powder

Filling
    900g cream cheese
    250ml double cream
    100g caster sugar
    100g light brown sugar
    20g plain flour
    2 medium-sized oranges, zest and juice
    200g dark cooking chocolate

Topping:
    Chocolate orange grated (optional)
    Chocolate orange slices (optional)

Instructions:

1.Prepare the Biscuits

- Place the digestive biscuits in a food processor and blitz them to fine crumbs.

2. Melt the Butter

- In a saucepan or microwave-safe bowl, melt the unsalted butter.

3. Combine Biscuits, Sugar, Cocoa Powder and Butter

- In the food processor combine the biscuit crumbs with the caster sugar and the cocoa powder, giving it a brief mix to ensure everything is combined. Add the melted butter to this mixture.

4. Mix Thoroughly

- Blitz the ingredients together for a few seconds in the food processor until the biscuit crumbs are evenly coated with the melted butter, cocoa powder and sugar. The mixture should resemble damp sand.

5. Prepare the Tin

- Take a 9-inch springform tin, which should be sprayed and lined.
- Pour the biscuit mixture into the base of the tin, and spread it out evenly, using a fork. Use the back of a spoon or the bottom of a glass to compact the mixture. Keep the pressure light but firm.

6. Chill the Base

- Place the tin in the refrigerator and let the base chill for 20 minutes or so. This helps the butter solidify, creating a firm foundation for your cheesecake.

7. Preheat the Oven

- Preheat your oven to 170°C.

8. Melt the Dark Chocolate

- In a glass bowl, break the 200g of dark chocolate into small chunks. Place the glass bowl over a pot of simmering water. Or, melt the chocolate in the microwave.

9. Prepare the Cream Cheese

- In a large mixing bowl, place the cream cheese. Ensure it's at room temperature for smoother blending. If at all possible, buy your cream cheese the day before baking, and leave it out of the refrigerator overnight. Ad the double cream to the cream cheese.

10. Add the Caster Sugar, LIght Brown Sugar and Flour

- Add the Caster Sugar, Light Brown Sugar and Flour to the Cream Cheese.

11. Zest and juice two oranges

- Firstly, use a grater to zest both oranges, before slicing them in half and using a lemon squeezer to extract the juice from all four halves of the oranges. Add both the zest and the juice to the cheesecake mix.

12. Blend Smoothly

- Use a hand mixer or a stand mixer to blend the ingredients together. Mix until the texture is smooth and all ingredients are well combined. Ensure there are no lumps.

13. Add the eggs

- Add the eggs, preferably one at a time, and scraping down the sides as you go, ensuring any unmixed ingredients are incorporated into the mix.

14. Add the melted dark chocolate to the cheesecake mix

- Because chocolate can be difficult to work with, this stage requires some care. Taking a large dessert spoon, add three spoonfuls of cream cheese mix to the melted chocolate in the bowl. Mix these together thoroughly by hand, before adding another three spoonfuls to the chocolate mix. Again, mix these together thoroughly by hand, and repeat this process until the entire cheesecake mix has been incorporated into the chocolate. I then usually pour everything back into the original cheesecake mixing bowl and give it one final blitz before pouring it out into the base.

15. Pour onto the Base

- Once your chocolate cheesecake base has chilled, pour the chocolate orange cream cheese filling onto it, spreading it evenly, smoothing the top with a spoon.

16. Wrap and Bake

- Wrap the tin in silver foil, then clingfilm, then sliver foil, as per my suggestion in the Bain Marie section of this book.
- Bake at 170°C for an hour, or until somewhat brown on top but still wobbly in the centre. Once it reaches it's optimum state of being cooked, the cake should 'puff up' above the top of the tin, something that will drop as soon as you take the cake out of the oven. If you feel it requires longer, give it a little more time in the oven.

17. Cool and Chill

- After baking, open the oven door and allow the cheesecake to cool slightly. When ready, remove it from the oven and the Bain Marie, and allow it to cool to room temperature, preferably on a wire rack.
- Cover and refrigerate for at least eight hours, or preferably overnight before serving.

-

26

STRAWBERRY ETON MESS

Anyone for tennis? And cheesecake?! Indulge in the delightful fusion of two classics with our Strawberry Eton Mess Cheese-cake.

Imagine a velvety cheesecake, each bite a celebration of creamy richness, paired with the vibrant freshness of ripe strawberries. A nod to the beloved Eton Mess, this dessert features swirls of strawberry coulis and airy clouds of whipped cream, adding layers of texture and flavor.

Nestled on a buttery biscuit base, this cheesecake promises a symphony of tastes – a perfect marriage of strawberries, cream, and the indulgent charm of cheesecake. Ideal for those seeking a delightful twist on tradition, our Strawberry Eton Mess Cheesecake is a treat to savor on any occasion.

If you want, you can make your own meringues to break up and mix into the topping. But I say, when they are so readily available in all supermarkets, why stress yourself out?

Base

260g digestive biscuits

90g unsalted butter
10g caster sugar

Filling
900g Cream Cheese
300ml double cream
200g strawberries, hulled and blitzed to juice
80g caster sugar
1 tsp vanilla extract
30g plain flour
4 eggs

Topping
300ml double cream, whipped
100g strawberries, hulled and sliced into small chunks
4 small plain meringue nests

Instructions:

1. Prepare the Biscuits

- Place the digestive biscuits in a food processor.
- Pulse the biscuits into fine crumbs.

2. Melt the Butter

- In a saucepan or microwave-safe bowl, melt the unsalted butter.

3. Combine Biscuits and Butter

- In the food processor, combine the biscuit crumbs with the caster sugar. Add the melted butter to this mixture.

4. Mix Thoroughly

- Blitz the ingredients together for a few seconds until the biscuit crumbs are evenly coated with the melted butter and sugar. The mixture should resemble damp sand.

5. Prepare the Tin

- Take a 9-inch springform tin, which should be sprayed and lined.
- Pour the biscuit mixture into the base of the tin, and spread it out evenly, using a fork. Use the back of a spoon or the bottom of a glass to compact the mixture. Keep the pressure light but firm.

6. Chill the Base

- Place the tin in the refrigerator and let the base chill for 20 minutes or so. This helps the butter solidify, creating a firm foundation for your cheesecake.

7. Preheat the Oven

- Preheat your oven to 160°C.

8. Prepare the Cream Cheese

- In a large mixing bowl, place the cream cheese. Ensure it's at

room temperature for smoother blending. If at all possible, buy your cream cheese the day before baking, and leave it out of the refrigerator overnight. Add the double cream to the cream cheese.

9. Blitz the Strawberries to a fine liquid and add them to the mix

- Remove the stems from 200g of strawberries and then blitz the fruit in the food processor until it simply resembles strawberry sauce. Pour the mix into the cream cheese.

10. Incorporate Sugar

- Sprinkle the caster sugar into the bowl with the cream cheese and condensed milk.

11. Add Vanilla Extract

- Add the teaspoon of vanilla extract to the mixture.

12. Sift in Flour

- Sift the plain flour into the bowl to avoid any lumps in the filling.

13. Blend Smoothly

- Use a hand mixer or a stand mixer to blend the ingredients together. Mix until the texture is smooth and all ingredients are well combined. Ensure there are no lumps.

14. Add the eggs

- Add the eggs, preferably one at a time, and scraping down the sides as you go, ensuring any unmixed ingredients are incorporated into the mix.

15. Pour onto the Base

- Once your cheesecake base has chilled, pour the cream cheese filling onto it, spreading it evenly, smoothing the top with a spoon.

16. Wrap and Bake

- Wrap the tin in silver foil, then clingfilm, then sliver foil, as per my suggestion in the Bain Marie section of this book.
- Bake at 160°C for an hour, or until golden brown on top but still wobbly in the centre. If you feel it requires longer, give it a little more time in the oven, but be careful not to burn this cake. I find that strawberries, cooked in the oven, can burn if you are not careful. Once it reaches it's optimum state of being cooked, the cake should 'puff up' above the top of the tin, something that will drop as soon as you take the cake out of the oven.

17. Cool and Chill

- After baking, open the oven door and allow the cheesecake to cool slightly. When ready, remove it from the oven and the Bain Marie, and allow it to cool to room temperature, preferably on a wire rack.

- Cover and refrigerate for at least eight hours, or preferably overnight before serving.

18. Prepare the Eton Mess Topping

- Remove the set cheesecake from the fridge and, using one or two pieces of kitchen roll, remove any moisture from the top of the cake that may have formed during the cooling process.
- Beat 300ml of double cream in a bowl until it is completely stiff.
- Smash the shop bought meringue nests into small pieces and add this to the whipped double cream.
- Hull and slice 100g of strawberries into small chunks, and add this to the whipped cream and smashed meringue.
- Gently fold the whipped double cream, meringue and strawberries together until they are nicely mixed. This should only take a few seconds.
- Add this to the top of the cake, and either serve immediately, or return to the fridge before serving.

27

PIMMS

Embrace the quintessential flavors of summer with our Pimm's Cheesecake, where the velvety richness of cheesecake harmonizes with the lively spirit of Pimm's liquor.

The smooth, indulgent texture seamlessly marries with a buttery biscuit base, creating a delightful treat that encapsulates the carefree vibes of sun-soaked days. Perfect for warm summer moments, this dessert offers a refreshing and flavorful indulgence, ideal for leisurely picnics under the sun.

As you gather with friends and family, our Pimm's Cheesecake promises to be the star of the spread, bringing a spirited essence to your summer picnic, making every bite a celebration of the season's delights.

Base
  260g digestive biscuits
  90g unsalted butter
  10g caster sugar

Filling

800g Cream Cheese
200ml double cream
3 shots Pimms
100g caster sugar
Zest & Juice 1 lemon
Zest & Juice 1 Orange
3 mint leaves diced
30g Flour
4 eggs

Topping
1 gelatine leaf
100 ml Pimms
20g caster sugar

Instructions:

1. Prepare the Biscuits

- Place the digestive biscuits in a food processor.
- Pulse the biscuits into fine crumbs.

2. Melt the Butter

- In a saucepan or microwave-safe bowl, melt the unsalted butter.

3. Combine Biscuits and Butter

- In the food processor, combine the biscuit crumbs with the caster sugar. Add the melted butter to this mixture.

4. Mix Thoroughly

- Blitz the ingredients together for a few seconds until the biscuit crumbs are evenly coated with the melted butter and sugar. The mixture should resemble damp sand.

5. Prepare the Tin

- Take a 9-inch springform tin, which should be sprayed and lined.
- Pour the biscuit mixture into the base of the tin, and spread it out evenly, using a fork. Use the back of a spoon or the bottom of a glass to compact the mixture. Keep the pressure light but firm.

6. Chill the Base

- Place the tin in the refrigerator and let the base chill for 20 minutes or so. This helps the butter solidify, creating a firm foundation for your cheesecake.

7. Preheat the Oven

- Preheat your oven to 160°C.

8. Prepare the Cream Cheese

- In a large mixing bowl, place the cream cheese. Ensure it's at room temperature for smoother blending. If at all possible, buy your cream cheese the day before baking, and leave it out of the refrigerator overnight. Add double cream to the mix.

9. Add 2 shots of PImms

- Using a shot glass, add 3 shots of Pimms (or 130ml of liquor if you don't have shot glasses lying around).

10. Incorporate Sugar

- Sprinkle the caster sugar into the bowl with the cream cheese and PImms.

11. Add the Zest and Juice of the fruit

- Firstly, zest both the orange and the lemon, using a grater. Then, slice both fruits in half and, using a lemon squeezer, squeeze the four segments of fruit separately, adding the juice of both to the cream cheese mix. Dice the mint leaves finely, and also add those to the mix.

12. Sift in Flour

- Sift the plain flour into the bowl to avoid any lumps in the filling.

13. Blend Smoothly

- Use a hand mixer or a stand mixer to blend the ingredients together. Mix until the texture is smooth and all ingredients are well combined. Ensure there are no lumps.

14. Add the eggs

- Add the eggs, preferably one at a time, and scraping down the sides as you go, ensuring any unmixed ingredients are incorporated into the mix.

15. Pour onto the Base

- Once your cheesecake base has chilled, pour the cream cheese filling onto it, spreading it evenly, smoothing the top with a spoon.

16. Wrap and Bake

- Wrap the tin in silver foil, then clingfilm, then sliver foil, as per my suggestion in the Bain Marie section of this book.
- Bake at 160°C for an hour, or until golden brown on top but still wobbly in the centre. If you feel it requires longer, give it a little more time in the oven, but be aware this is quite a wet cake, so it might need a little longer. Once it reaches it's optimum state of being cooked, the cake should 'puff up' above the top of the tin, something that will drop as soon as you take the cake out of the oven.

17. Cool and Chill

- After baking, open the oven door and allow the cheesecake to cool slightly. When ready, remove it from the oven and the Bain Marie, and allow it to cool to room temperature, preferably on a wire rack.
- Cover and refrigerate for at least eight hours, or preferably

overnight before adding the topping.

18. Preparing the topping

- Prepare the gelatine leaf by soaking the the sheet in cold water according to package instructions until it becomes soft and pliable.
- Heat 100ml of Pimms and 20g of caster sugar in a glass bowl over a gently simmering pot of water until it is warm.
- Squeeze any excess water from the soaked gelatine sheet and add it to the mixture. Stir until the gelatine dissolves completely.
- Allow the topping mixture to cool for a few moments before pouring it over the baked and set cheesecake. This step ensures a smooth and even distribution of the topping.
- Place the cheesecake with the topping back into the refrigerator to allow it to set completely. This should take approximately two hours, before the cake is ready to serve.

Serve with freshly sliced strawberries on top.

PIMM'S
No1

28

APPLE & BLACKBERRY CRUMBLE

Delight in the creation of this, our Apple and Blackberry Crumble Cheesecake, a culinary masterpiece where velvety cheesecake meets the rich sweetness of baked apples and the tart allure of plump blackberries.

Resting on a buttery biscuit base, this dessert is adorned with a generous layer of crumble topping, adding a delightful contrast of textures. Each bite becomes a symphony of creamy richness, fruity sweetness, and the satisfying crunch of crumble.

Perfect for those who crave the nostalgic charm of a classic crumble, this Apple and Blackberry Crumble Cheesecake is a delightful fusion, crafted to satisfy your dessert cravings, with the crumble topping serving as the pièce de résistance.

This was always usually one of the first cakes to sell out at our various food markets. You can, if you wish, leave out the blackberries, and just have it the good old fashioned way with apples by themselves. Crimble-crumble!

Base

260g digestive biscuits

90g unsalted butter

10g caster sugar

Filling

900g Cream Cheese

250ml double cream

1 tsp vanilla extract

120g caster sugar

30g flour

2 Bramley Apples

150g blackberries sautéed

1/4tsp nutmeg

4 eggs

Crumble Topping

110g plain flour

110g light soft brown sugar

1/2tsp cinnamon

75g cold unsalted butter, diced

Instructions:

1. Prepare the Biscuits

- Place the digestive biscuits in a food processor.
- Pulse the biscuits into fine crumbs.

2. Melt the Butter

- In a saucepan or microwave-safe bowl, melt the unsalted butter.

3. Combine Biscuits and Butter

- In the food processor, combine the biscuit crumbs with the caster sugar. Add the melted butter to this mixture.

4. Mix Thoroughly

- Blitz the ingredients together for a few seconds until the biscuit crumbs are evenly coated with the melted butter and sugar. The mixture should resemble damp sand.

5. Prepare the Tin

- Take a 9-inch springform tin, which should be sprayed and lined.
- Pour the biscuit mixture into the base of the tin, and spread it out evenly, using a fork. Use the back of a spoon or the bottom of a glass to compact the mixture. Keep the pressure light but firm.

6. Chill the Base

- Place the tin in the refrigerator and let the base chill for 20 minutes or so. This helps the butter solidify, creating a firm foundation for your cheesecake.

7. Preheat the Oven

- Preheat your oven to 160°C.

8. Prepare the Cream Cheese

- In a large mixing bowl, place the cream cheese. Ensure it's at room temperature for smoother blending. If at all possible, buy your cream cheese the day before baking, and leave it out of the refrigerator overnight. Add the double cream .

9. Add Vanilla Extract

- Add one teaspoon of Vanilla Extract.

10. Incorporate Sugar

- Sprinkle the caster sugar into the bowl with the cream cheese.

11. Sift in Flour

- Sift the plain flour into the bowl to avoid any lumps in the filling.

12. Blend Smoothly

- Use a hand mixer or a stand mixer to blend the ingredients together. Mix until the texture is smooth and all ingredients are well combined. Ensure there are no lumps.

13. Add the eggs

- Add the eggs, preferably one at a time, and scraping down the sides as you go, ensuring any unmixed ingredients are incorporated into the mix.

14. Prepare the fruit

- Simply core, peel and thinly slice the 2 Bramley Apples. Sauté the blackberries, simply by heating them in a saucepan with a little water and a pinch of caster sugar, until they resemble a thick sauce.

15. Pour onto the Base and add the fruit

- Once your cheesecake base has chilled, pour approximately half the cream cheese filling onto it. Then, cover the entire surface with the Bramley Apple Slices. Then, spread the blackberry sauce all over these, almost until it reaches the edge of tin. Then, sprinkle ¼ teaspoon of nutmeg over the fruit. Then, pour the remaining cheesecake batter over the fruit, spreading it evenly, smoothing the top with a spoon.

16. Make the crumble

- Prepare the crumble mixture by combining the plain flour and soft brown sugar in a mixing bowl. Sprinkle in the pinch of cinnamon and ensure an even mix. Then add the cold, diced butter into the mixture, using your fingertips to create a texture like coarse breadcrumbs. Evenly spread the crumble mixture over the top of the cheesecake mixture, using a dessert spoon to both distribute the crumbs and press them down lightly.

17. Wrap and Bake

- Wrap the tin in silver foil, then clingfilm, then sliver foil, as

per my suggestion in the Bain Marie section of this book.
- Bake at 160°C for an hour and a quarter, or until the crumble is golden brown on top but still wobbly in the centre. If you feel it requires longer, give it a little more time in the oven, especially as it can take time for the heat to penetrate the crumble and cook the cheesecake underneath. Once it reaches it's optimum state of being cooked, the cake should 'puff up' above the top of the tin, something that will drop as soon as you take the cake out of the oven.

18. Cool and Chill

- After baking, open the oven door and allow the cheesecake to cool slightly. When ready, remove it from the oven and the Bain Marie, and allow it to cool to room temperature, preferably on a wire rack.
- Cover and refrigerate for at least eight hours, or preferably overnight before serving.

Serve with single pouring cream or vanilla ice-cream.

29

CHOCOLATE BROWNIE

Prepare to embark on a baking journey with our irresistible Chocolate Brownie Cheesecake – a true delight for enthusiasts of both brownies and cheesecake. As you gather your ingredients and preheat the oven, envision the decadent fusion taking place: the rich intensity of chocolate brownie marvelously woven into the velvety embrace of the cheesecake, all without the need for a traditional base.

Picture the kitchen transforming into a haven of aromas as the luscious batter comes together, creating a symphony of flavors that promises to redefine your dessert expectations. With each luxurious bite, celebrate the harmonious union between the creamy cheesecake texture and the dense, gooey allure of chocolate brownie. This creation transcends the boundaries of traditional desserts, offering a sensory experience that captures the essence of pure indulgence.

For those who relish a no-frills, full-chocolate experience, our Chocolate Brownie Cheesecake is a culinary masterpiece that satisfies your sweet cravings with unparalleled richness. As you navigate the baking process, imagine the anticipation building, knowing that the end result will be a symphony of textures and flavors that elevates your dessert game to new heights.

So, let the oven work its magic, let the aromas fill your kitchen, and anticipate a culinary adventure that culminates in a Chocolate Brownie Cheesecake – a creation that seamlessly marries two beloved treats into a single, irresistible masterpiece. May each mouthful be a celebration of your baking prowess and a journey into the pure decadence of this delectable fusion.

Brownie:
    100g unsalted butter
    150g dark chocolate
    100g caster sugar
    100g dark brown sugar
    2 eggs
    80g flour

Cheesecake:
    800g Cream Cheese
    100g caster sugar
    20g flour
    1 tsp Vanilla Extract
    2 eggs
    100g milk chocolate chips

Instructions:

1. Start by making the Brownie Mix

- Place 100g of unsalted butter in a large mixing bowl with 150g of dark chocolate and melt them slowly together over a pan of simmering water. Once melted, mix them together gently to form a silky texture.

2. Beat the eggs with the sugars

- In a separate mixing bowl, place the caster sugar with the dark brown sugar, and add two eggs. Beat with an electric whisk until the volume doubles in size. This may take several minutes.

3. Mix together

- Once the dark chocolate and butter have melted, remove them from the heat and pour them into the sugary egg mixture.

4. Add flour

- Now add 80g of plain flour to the mix and gently combine them until you end up with a thick brownie mix. Set this aside and make the cheesecake batter.

5. Preheat the Oven

- Preheat your oven to 160ºC.

6. Prepare the Cream Cheese

- In a large mixing bowl, place the cream cheese. Ensure it's at room temperature for smoother blending. If at all possible, buy your cream cheese the day before baking, and leave it out of the refrigerator overnight.

7. Add Vanilla Extract

- Add one teaspoon of Vanilla Extract.

8. Incorporate Sugar

- Sprinkle the caster sugar into the bowl with the cream cheese.

9. Sift in Flour

- Sift the plain flour into the bowl to avoid any lumps in the filling.

10. Blend Smoothly

- Use a hand mixer or a stand mixer to blend the ingredients together. Mix until the texture is smooth and all ingredients are well combined. Ensure there are no lumps.

11. Add the eggs

- Add the eggs, preferably one at a time, and scraping down the sides as you go, ensuring any unmixed ingredients are incorporated into the mix.

12. Add the milk chocolate drops

- Fold the milk chocolate drops into the cheesecake batter.

13. Fold the cheesecake batter into the brownie mix

- Now, using a spatula or wooden spoon, fold the cheesecake batter casually into the brownie mix, creating as much of a marbling effect as you can manage. Do not overly mix the two together, as you will end up with no discernible difference between cheesecake and brownie if you do so.

14. Prepare the Tin

- Take a 9-inch springform tin, which should be sprayed and lined.

15. Pour into the tin

- Pour the Chocolate Brownie Cheesecake filling into the tin, spreading it evenly, smoothing the top with a spoon. If necessary, use a knife to swirl the brownie mixture further into the cheesecake mix.

16. Wrap and Bake

- Wrap the tin in silver foil, then clingfilm, then sliver foil, as per my suggestion in the Bain Marie section of this book.
- Bake at 160°C for an hour, or until golden brown on top but still wobbly in the centre. Once it reaches it's optimum state of being cooked, the cake should 'puff up' above the top of the tin, something that will drop as soon as you take the cake out of the oven.

17. Cool and Chill

- After baking, open the oven door and allow the cheesecake to cool slightly. When ready, remove it from the oven and the Bain Marie, and allow it to cool to room temperature, preferably on a wire rack.
- Cover and refrigerate for at least eight hours, or preferably overnight.

Serve with fresh raspberries and pouring cream. Or chocolate ice-cream.

30

RED VELVET

Delight in the enchanting blend of flavors with our Red Velvet Cheesecake. If you're a fan of both red velvet and chocolate, you're in for a treat.

Imagine a velvety cheesecake infused with the iconic taste of red velvet, where the rich cocoa meets a hint of buttermilk tang. Nestled on a chocolate biscuit base, each luxurious bite is a symphony of textures and tastes.

Topped with a luscious cream cheese frosting, this dessert is a celebration of the classic red velvet allure, perfect for those who appreciate the perfect harmony of creamy cheesecake and the distinctive charm of red velvet cake.

Base
  250g digestive biscuits
  90g unsalted butter
  10g caster sugar
  15g cocoa powder

900g Cream Cheese

200g caster sugar
50g flour
130ml buttermilk
30g cocoa powder
1 tsp strong red food colouring
4 eggs

Icing
100g butter
250g icing sugar
100g cream cheese
1 tsp Vanilla extract

Instructions:

1.Prepare the Biscuits

- Place the digestive biscuits in a food processor and blitz them to fine crumbs.

2. Melt the Butter

- In a saucepan or microwave-safe bowl, melt the unsalted butter.

3. Combine Biscuits, Sugar, Cocoa Powder and Butter

- In the food processor combine the biscuit crumbs with the caster sugar and the cocoa powder, giving it a brief mix to ensure everything is combined. Add the melted butter to this mixture.

4. Mix Thoroughly

- Blitz the ingredients together for a few seconds in the food processor until the biscuit crumbs are evenly coated with the melted butter, cocoa powder and sugar. The mixture should resemble damp sand.

5. Prepare the Tin

- Take a 9-inch springform tin, which should be sprayed and lined.
- Pour the biscuit mixture into the base of the tin, and spread it out evenly, using a fork. Use the back of a spoon or the bottom of a glass to compact the mixture. Keep the pressure light but firm.

6. Chill the Base

- Place the tin in the refrigerator and let the base chill for 20 minutes or so. This helps the butter solidify, creating a firm foundation for your cheesecake.

7. Preheat the Oven

- Preheat your oven to 170ºC.

8. Prepare the Cream Cheese

- In a large mixing bowl, place the cream cheese. Ensure it's at room temperature for smoother blending. If at all possible, buy your cream cheese the day before baking, and leave it out of the refrigerator overnight.

9. Add the Caster Sugar, Flour and Buttermilk

- Add the Caster Sugar, Flour and Buttermilk to the Cream Cheese, before blending smoothly.

10. Add the cocoa powder and red food colouring

- Now add the cocoa powder and red food colouring to the mix.

11. Blend Smoothly

- Blend the ingredients together. Mix until the texture is smooth and all ingredients are well combined. Ensure there are no lumps. In addition, ensure the mixture is 'red' enough for you. If not, add a little more food colouring, ensuring it is fully incorporated into the mix.

12. Add the eggs

- Add the eggs, preferably one at a time, and scraping down the sides as you go, ensuring any unmixed ingredients are incorporated into the mix.

13. Pour onto the Base

- Once your chocolate cheesecake base has chilled, pour the Red Velvet cream cheese filling onto it, spreading it evenly, smoothing the top with a spoon.

14. Wrap and Bake

- Wrap the tin in silver foil, then clingfilm, then sliver foil, as per my suggestion in the Bain Marie section of this book.
- Bake at 170°C for an hour and twenty minutes, or until somewhat brown on top but still wobbly in the centre. If you feel it requires longer, give it a little more time in the oven. This is a very wet cake, owing to the Buttermilk, so it can require longer at times. Once it reaches it's optimum state of being cooked, the cake should 'puff up' above the top of the tin, something that will drop as soon as you take the cake out of the oven.

15. Cool and Chill

- After baking, open the oven door and allow the cheesecake to cool slightly. When ready, remove it from the oven and the Bain Marie, and allow it to cool to room temperature, preferably on a wire rack.
- Cover and refrigerate for at least eight hours, or preferably overnight before adding the topping.

16. Make the Cream Cheese Frosting

- Start by ensuring the butter is at room temperature for easy blending. In a mixing bowl, beat 100g of softened butter until it is one smooth, gooey mass of butter. Now add 250g of icing sugar. Beat the mixture until it turns light and fluffy.
- Gradually incorporate 100g of cream cheese into the fluffy butter and sugar mixture, continuing to beat until the frosting achieves a smooth consistency. Finally, add a

teaspoon of vanilla extract. Blend the ingredients well.

· Remove the cheesecake from the fridge and remove any excess moisture with a kitchen towel or two.

· Spread the cream cheese frosting over the top of the cake in an even pattern, smoothing the top with a spoon.

· Return the cake to the fridge for an hour or so, in order for the frosting to harden before serving.

31

KEY LIME

Savour the tropical allure of this, our Key Lime Cheesecake, a delightful fusion of velvety cheesecake and the bold, tangy essence of fresh key limes.

Resting on a buttery graham digestive biscuit crust, each sumptuous bite is a symphony of creamy indulgence and citrusy brightness. This cheesecake skips the traditional topping, allowing the pure flavors of key lime and creamy cheesecake to take center stage.

For those who appreciate a straightforward and refreshing dessert, this Key Lime Cheesecake is a perfect balance of sweetness and zest, bringing a taste of the sunshine state to every delightful slice.

Base
  260g digestive biscuits
  90g unsalted butter
  10g caster sugar

Filling

900g Cream Cheese
300ml double cream
1 tin of condensed milk
3 limes zest
6 limes juiced
40g plain flour
4 eggs

Instructions:

1. Prepare the Biscuits

- Place the digestive biscuits in a food processor.
- Pulse the biscuits into fine crumbs.

2. Melt the Butter

- In a saucepan or microwave-safe bowl, melt the unsalted butter.

3. Combine Biscuits and Butter

- In the food processor, combine the biscuit crumbs with the caster sugar. Add the melted butter to this mixture.

4. Mix Thoroughly

- Blitz the ingredients together for a few seconds until the biscuit crumbs are evenly coated with the melted butter and sugar. The mixture should resemble damp sand.

5. Prepare the Tin

- Take a 9-inch springform tin, which should be sprayed and lined.
- Pour the biscuit mixture into the base of the tin, and spread it out evenly, using a fork. Use the back of a spoon or the bottom of a glass to compact the mixture. Keep the pressure light but firm.

6. Chill the Base

- Place the tin in the refrigerator and let the base chill for 20 minutes or so. This helps the butter solidify, creating a firm foundation for your cheesecake. Once it has set, remove the tin from the fridge, and slather approximately 1 tablespoon of lemon curd over the base, ensuring a well covered, yet thin coating. Return the tin to the fridge.

7. Preheat the Oven

- Preheat your oven to 160°C.

8. Prepare the Cream Cheese

- In a large mixing bowl, place the cream cheese. Ensure it's at room temperature for smoother blending. If at all possible, buy your cream cheese the day before baking, and leave it out of the refrigerator overnight. Add the double cream to the cream cheese.

9. Add the Condensed Milk

- Open the tin of condensed milk and add it to the cream cheese.

10. Add Lime Zest and Juice

- Using a grater, finely zest the outside of 3 limes into the cream cheese mix. Then slice all 6 limes in half. Then, using a lemon squeezer, squeeze the juice of all twelve of the lime halves into the cheesecake mix.

11. Sift in Flour

- Sift the plain flour into the bowl to avoid any lumps in the filling.

12. Blend Smoothly

- Use a hand mixer or a stand mixer to blend the ingredients together. Mix until the texture is smooth and all ingredients are well combined. Ensure there are no lumps.

13. Add the eggs

- Add the eggs, preferably one at a time, and scraping down the sides as you go, ensuring any unmixed ingredients are incorporated into the mix.

14. Pour onto the Base

- Once your cheesecake base has chilled and the lemon curd has set a little, pour the cream cheese filling onto it, spreading it evenly, smoothing the top with a spoon.

15. Wrap and Bake

- Wrap the tin in silver foil, then clingfilm, then sliver foil, as per my suggestion in the Bain Marie section of this book.
- Bake at 160°C for an hour, or until golden brown on top but still wobbly in the centre. If you feel it requires longer, give it a little more time in the oven. Once it reaches it's optimum state of being cooked, the cake should 'puff up' above the top of the tin, something that will drop as soon as you take the cake out of the oven.

16. Cool and Chill

- After baking, open the oven door and allow the cheesecake to cool slightly. When ready, remove it from the oven and the Bain Marie, and allow it to cool to room temperature, preferably on a wire rack.
- Cover and refrigerate for at least eight hours, or preferably overnight before serving.
- Top with freshly whipped double cream, and pipe over the top of the cake with a little grated lime zest if possible.

32

COFFEE

Awaken your taste buds with this, my Coffee Cheesecake, a delightful fusion of velvety cheesecake and the rich, robust essence of coffee.

Picture a creamy indulgence that captures the aromatic notes of freshly brewed coffee, all nestled on a buttery biscuit crust, to which you can add walnuts, should you wish. Each decadent bite offers a perfect balance of creamy texture and the invigorating kick of coffee, making it an ideal treat for coffee enthusiasts.

Whether enjoyed as an indulgent dessert or a delightful pick-me-up, this Coffee Cheesecake promises a satisfying experience for those who appreciate the harmonious pairing of creamy sweetness and the bold flavor of coffee.

Base
   250g digestive biscuits
   50g walnuts (optional)
   90g unsalted butter
   10g caster sugar

Filling
  900g Cream Cheese
  300ml double cream
  3 tablespoons instant coffee
  1 tsp Vanilla extract
  120g caster sugar
  20g plain flour
  4 eggs

Instructions:

1. Prepare the Biscuits (and walnuts if wanted)

- Place the digestive biscuits (and walnuts) in a food processor. If you do use walnuts, reduce the biscuits by 50g (making 200g in total).
- Pulse the biscuits into fine crumbs.

2. Melt the Butter

- In a saucepan or microwave-safe bowl, melt the unsalted butter.

3. Combine Biscuits and Butter

- In the food processor, combine the biscuit crumbs with the caster sugar. Add the melted butter to this mixture.

4. Mix Thoroughly

- Blitz the ingredients together for a few seconds until the biscuit crumbs are evenly coated with the melted butter and sugar. The mixture should resemble damp sand.

5. Prepare the Tin

- Take a 9-inch springform tin, which should be sprayed and lined.
- Pour the biscuit mixture into the base of the tin, and spread it out evenly, using a fork. Use the back of a spoon or the bottom of a glass to compact the mixture. Keep the pressure light but firm.

6. Chill the Base

- Place the tin in the refrigerator and let the base chill for 20 minutes or so. This helps the butter solidify, creating a firm foundation for your cheesecake.

7. Preheat the Oven

- Preheat your oven to 170ºC.

8. Prepare the Cream Cheese and Double Cream

- In a large mixing bowl, place the cream cheese. Ensure it's at room temperature for smoother blending. If at all possible, buy your cream cheese the day before baking, and leave it out of the refrigerator overnight. Add the double cream to the bowl of cream cheese.

9. Add the Coffee and Vanilla Extract

- Add three tablespoons of Instant Coffee and one teaspoon of Vanilla Extract to the cream cheese.

10. Incorporate Sugar

- Sprinkle the caster sugar into the bowl with the cream cheese.

11. Sift in Flour

- Sift the plain flour into the bowl to avoid any lumps in the filling.

12. Blend Smoothly

- Use a hand mixer or a stand mixer to blend the ingredients together. Mix until the texture is smooth and all ingredients are well combined. Ensure there are no lumps.

13. Add the eggs

- Add the eggs, preferably one at a time, and scraping down the sides as you go, ensuring any unmixed ingredients are incorporated into the mix.

14. Pour onto the Base

- Once your cheesecake base has chilled, pour the coffee cream cheese filling onto it, spreading it evenly, smoothing the top with a spoon.

15. Wrap and Bake

- Wrap the tin in silver foil, then clingfilm, then sliver foil, as per my suggestion in the Bain Marie section of this book.
- Bake at 170°C for an hour, or until golden brown on top but still wobbly in the centre. If you feel it requires longer, give it a little more time in the oven. Once it reaches it's optimum state of being cooked, the cake should 'puff up' above the top of the tin, something that will drop as soon as you take the cake out of the oven.

16. Cool and Chill

- After baking, open the oven door and allow the cheesecake to cool slightly. When ready, remove it from the oven and the Bain Marie, and allow it to cool to room temperature, preferably on a wire rack.
- Cover and refrigerate for at least eight hours, or preferably overnight before serving.
- Serve with a little whipped cream and chocolate shavings (optional).

33

BANANA CREAM PIE

Delight in the amalgamation of two classic desserts with our Banana Cream Pie Cheesecake. Envision a velvety cheesecake, skillfully infused with the inherent sweetness of ripe bananas, resting atop a buttery digestive biscuit crust. Every bite offers a harmonious marriage of creamy indulgence and the comforting nostalgia associated with banana cream pie.

As you savor this exquisite creation, consider the carefully balanced layers that contribute to its overall appeal. Crowned with a luscious layer of whipped cream, the dessert achieves a perfect equilibrium of textures and flavors.

Whether your preference leans towards the smooth allure of cheesecake or the familiar embrace of banana cream pie, this creation thoughtfully brings the best of both worlds to your palate. It assures a gratifying experience, where the subtle richness of digestive biscuits adds depth to the delicate sweetness of ripe bananas, resulting in a straightforward yet indulgent treat that pays homage to these timeless favorites.

Base

260g digestive biscuits
90g unsalted butter
10g caster sugar

Filling
900g Cream Cheese
300ml double cream
1 tin condensed milk
40g caster sugar
1 tsp vanilla paste
35g plain flour
4 large ripe bananas, pulped to mush
4 eggs

Instructions:

1. Prepare the Biscuits

- Place the digestive biscuits in a food processor.
- Pulse the biscuits into fine crumbs.

2. Melt the Butter

- In a saucepan or microwave-safe bowl, melt the unsalted butter.

3. Combine Biscuits and Butter

- In the food processor, combine the biscuit crumbs with the caster sugar. Add the melted butter to this mixture.

4. Mix Thoroughly

- Blitz the ingredients together for a few seconds until the biscuit crumbs are evenly coated with the melted butter and sugar. The mixture should resemble damp sand.

5. Prepare the Tin

- Take a 9-inch springform tin, which should be sprayed and lined.
- Pour the biscuit mixture into the base of the tin, and spread it out evenly, using a fork. Use the back of a spoon or the bottom of a glass to compact the mixture. Keep the pressure light but firm.

6. Chill the Base

- Place the tin in the refrigerator and let the base chill for 20 minutes or so. This helps the butter solidify, creating a firm foundation for your cheesecake.

7. Preheat the Oven

- Preheat your oven to 170°C.

8. Prepare the Cream Cheese and Double Cream

- In a large mixing bowl, place the cream cheese. Ensure it's at room temperature for smoother blending. If at all possible, buy your cream cheese the day before baking, and leave it out of the refrigerator overnight. Add the double cream to the bowl of cream cheese.

9. Add the Condensed Milk

- Open the tin of condensed milk and add it to the cream cheese.

10. Incorporate Sugar

- Sprinkle the caster sugar into the bowl with the cream cheese and condensed milk.

11. Add Vanilla Paste

- Add the teaspoon of vanilla paste to the mixture.

12. Sift in Flour

- Sift the plain flour into the bowl to avoid any lumps in the filling.

13. Pulp the bananas

- Pulp the 4 ripe bananas in a food processor until they are smooth mush, like a smoothie. Add them to the bowl of cream cheese.

14. Blend Smoothly

- Use a hand mixer or a stand mixer to blend the ingredients together. Mix until the texture is smooth and all ingredients are well combined. Ensure there are no lumps.

15. Add the eggs

- Add the eggs, preferably one at a time, and scraping down the sides as you go, ensuring any unmixed ingredients are incorporated into the mix.

16. Pour onto the Base

- Once your cheesecake base has chilled, pour the cream cheese filling onto it, spreading it evenly, smoothing the top with a spoon.

17. Wrap and Bake

- Wrap the tin in silver foil, then clingfilm, then sliver foil, as per my suggestion in the Bain Marie section of this book.
- Bake at 170°C for an hour, or until golden brown on top but still wobbly in the centre. If you feel it requires longer, give it a little more time in the oven. Once it reaches it's optimum state of being cooked, the cake should 'puff up' above the top of the tin, something that will drop as soon as you take the cake out of the oven.

18. Cool and Chill

- After baking, open the oven door and allow the cheesecake to cool slightly. When ready, remove it from the oven and the Bain Marie, and allow it to cool to room temperature, preferably on a wire rack.

· Cover and refrigerate for at least eight hours, or preferably overnight before serving.

Serve with whipped cream, either piped on top of the cake just before serving, or alongside.

34

TOBLERONE

Long before I ventured into the cheesecake business, I had the pleasure of experiencing the enchantment of this delectable dessert at a friend's dinner party. From that moment, I was instantly hooked. There's a certain allure in the decadence of this particular creation, where the velvety embrace of cheesecake intricately intertwines with the irresistibly smooth texture and satisfying crunch of Toblerone chocolate.

Imagine the artistry of this dessert unfolding as it rests on a rich chocolate biscuit base, setting the stage for a symphony of indulgence with every bite. The distinct flavor profile of Toblerone becomes the star, infusing each layer with a unique and delightful character. This cheesecake is a treat specifically tailored for chocolate enthusiasts, promising a delightful journey that explores the layers of creamy smoothness and the delectable crunch of Toblerone.

What makes this creation stand out is its ability to deliver a complete chocolate experience without the need for additional toppings. Each element, from the velvety cheesecake to the rich chocolate biscuit base and the distinctive Toblerone crunch, plays a crucial role in crafting a dessert that transcends the ordinary. So, long before my cheesecake business took flight, this Toblerone Chocolate Cheesecake left an indelible mark on my taste buds, and now, it's ready to captivate the palates of chocolate enthusiasts everywhere.

Base
    200g digestive biscuits
    50g almonds
    10g caster sugar
    15g cocoa powder
    90g unsalted butter

900g Cream Cheese
    300ml double cream
    120g caster sugar
    30g cocoa powder
    2 tbsps honey
    20g plain flour
    1 large Toblerone bar (360g), broken up and melted
    4 eggs

Instructions:

1.Prepare the Biscuits and Almonds

- Place the digestive biscuits in a food processor and blitz them to fine crumbs.

2. Melt the Butter

- In a saucepan or microwave-safe bowl, melt the unsalted butter.

3. Combine Biscuits, Almonds, Sugar, Cocoa Powder and Butter

- In the food processor combine the biscuit crumbs with the caster sugar and the cocoa powder, giving it a brief mix to ensure everything is combined. Add the melted butter to this mixture.

4. Mix Thoroughly

- Blitz the ingredients together for a few seconds in the food processor until the biscuit crumbs are evenly coated with the melted butter, cocoa powder and sugar. The mixture should resemble damp sand.

5. Prepare the Tin

- Take a 9-inch springform tin, which should be sprayed and lined.
- Pour the biscuit mixture into the base of the tin, and spread it out evenly, using a fork. Use the back of a spoon or the bottom of a glass to compact the mixture. Keep the pressure light but firm.

6. Chill the Base

- Place the tin in the refrigerator and let the base chill for 20 minutes or so. This helps the butter solidify, creating a firm foundation for your cheesecake.

7. Preheat the Oven

- Preheat your oven to 170°C.

8. Prepare the Cream Cheese and Double Cream

- In a large mixing bowl, place the cream cheese. Ensure it's at room temperature for smoother blending. If at all possible, buy your cream cheese the day before baking, and leave it out of the refrigerator overnight. Add the double cream to the cream cheese.

9. Add the Caster Sugar, Cocoa Powder, Honey and Flour

- Add the Caster Sugar, Cocoa Powder, Honey and Flour to the Cream Cheese, before blending smoothly.

10. Add the eggs

- Add the eggs, preferably one at a time, and scraping down the sides as you go, ensuring any unmixed ingredients are incorporated into the mix.

11. Melt the Toblerone bar and add it to the cheesecake mix

- Because chocolate can be difficult to work with, this stage requires some care. Firstly, melt the Toblerone bar in a bowl, placed over a pot of simmering water. Taking a large dessert spoon, add three spoonfuls of cream cheese mix to the melted Toblerone in the bowl. Mix these together thoroughly by hand, before adding another three spoonfuls to the Toblerone mix. Again, mix these together thoroughly by hand, and repeat this process until the entire cheesecake mix has been incorporated into the melted Toblerone.

12. Blend Smoothly

- Pour the Toblerone cheesecake mix back into the original bowl, and blend the ingredients together. Mix until the texture is smooth and all ingredients are well combined. Ensure there are no lumps.

13. Pour onto the Base

- Once your chocolate cheesecake almond base has chilled, pour the Toblerone cream cheese filling onto it, spreading it evenly, smoothing the top with a spoon.

14. Wrap and Bake

- Wrap the tin in silver foil, then clingfilm, then sliver foil, as per my suggestion in the Bain Marie section of this book.
- Bake at 170°C for an hour and twenty minutes, or until somewhat brown on top but still wobbly in the centre. If you feel it requires longer, give it a little more time in the oven. Once it reaches it's optimum state of being cooked, the cake should 'puff up' above the top of the tin, something that will drop as soon as you take the cake out of the oven.

15. Cool and Chill

- After baking, open the oven door and allow the cheesecake to cool slightly. When ready, remove it from the oven and the Bain Marie, and allow it to cool to room temperature, preferably on a wire rack.
- Cover and refrigerate for at least eight hours, or preferably overnight.

If possible, serve with gratings of Toblerone chocolate, although I prefer to eat it exactly as it is.

35

PUMPKIN

Without a doubt, this is one of the most fabulous cheesecakes I have ever had the pleasure of creating.

Embrace the warmth of the Halloween season with this, my Pumpkin Cheesecake, a delightful blend of velvety cheesecake and the comforting flavors of pumpkin. The vevelty pumpkin purée mixes with the cream cheese, perfectly spiced with autumnal notes, resting on a buttery digestive base. Each luxurious bite is a symphony of smooth texture and the distinct, cozy essence of pumpkin.

Whether enjoyed as a festive treat or a comforting dessert year-round, this Cheesecake captures the essence of Autumn in every delightful slice, making it a perfect indulgence for those who appreciate the harmonious blend of creamy sweetness and the nostalgic taste of pumpkin.

Base
  260g digestive biscuits
  ½ teaspoon ground nutmeg
  90g unsalted butter

10g caster sugar

Filling
    900g Cream Cheese
    200g pumpkin puree
    180g caster sugar
    1 tsp ground cinnamon
    30g plain flour
    4 eggs

Instructions:

1. Prepare the Biscuits

- Place the digestive biscuits in a food processor.
- Pulse the biscuits into fine crumbs.

2. Melt the Butter

- In a saucepan or microwave-safe bowl, melt the unsalted butter.

3. Combine Biscuits and Butter

- In the food processor, combine the biscuit crumbs with the caster sugar and the nutmeg. Add the melted butter to this mixture.

4. Mix Thoroughly

- Blitz the ingredients together for a few seconds until the biscuit crumbs are evenly coated with the melted butter and sugar. The mixture should resemble damp sand.

5. Prepare the Tin

- Take a 9-inch springform tin, which should be sprayed and lined.
- Pour the biscuit mixture into the base of the tin, and spread it out evenly, using a fork. Use the back of a spoon or the bottom of a glass to compact the mixture. Keep the pressure light but firm.

6. Chill the Base

- Place the tin in the refrigerator and let the base chill for 20 minutes or so. This helps the butter solidify, creating a firm foundation for your cheesecake.

7. Preheat the Oven

- Preheat your oven to 170°C.

8. Prepare the Cream Cheese

- In a large mixing bowl, place the cream cheese. Ensure it's at room temperature for smoother blending. If at all possible, buy your cream cheese the day before baking, and leave it out of the refrigerator overnight.

9. Add the Pumpkin Puree

- Open the tin of Pumpkin Puree and add it to the cream cheese.

10. Incorporate Sugar

- Sprinkle the caster sugar into the bowl with the cream cheese and puree.

11. Add Ground Cinammon

- Add the teaspoon of ground cinammon to the mixture.

12. Sift in Flour

- Sift the plain flour into the bowl to avoid any lumps in the filling.

13. Blend Smoothly

- Use a hand mixer or a stand mixer to blend the ingredients together. Mix until the texture is smooth and all ingredients are well combined. Ensure there are no lumps.

14. Add the eggs

- Add the eggs, preferably one at a time, and scraping down the sides as you go, ensuring any unmixed ingredients are incorporated into the mix.

15. Pour onto the Base

- Once your cheesecake base has chilled, pour the cream cheese filling onto it, spreading it evenly, smoothing the top with a spoon.

16. Wrap and Bake

- Wrap the tin in silver foil, then clingfilm, then sliver foil, as per my suggestion in the Bain Marie section of this book.
- Bake at 170°C for an hour, or until golden brown on top but still wobbly in the centre. If you feel it requires longer, give it a little more time in the oven. Once it reaches it's optimum state of being cooked, the cake should 'puff up' above the top of the tin, something that will drop as soon as you take the cake out of the oven.

17. Cool and Chill

- After baking, open the oven door and allow the cheesecake to cool slightly. When ready, remove it from the oven and the Bain Marie, and allow it to cool to room temperature, preferably on a wire rack.
- Cover and refrigerate for at least eight hours, or preferably overnight before serving.

36

MALTESERS

Experience the delightful fusion of velvety cheesecake and the rich malty flavor of Maltesers with this, our Maltesers Cheesecake.

Imagine a creamy texture seamlessly blended with the distinct taste of these iconic malted chocolate spheres, all resting on a chocolate biscuit base. Each sumptuous bite is a symphony of smoothness, creating a luscious dessert perfect for chocolate enthusiasts.

Topped with a generous layer of milk chocolate ganache, this cheesecake is a celebration of decadent sweetness, promising a delightful journey through layers of creamy indulgence and the irresistible charm of Maltesers.

Base
  250g digestive biscuits
  90g unsalted butter
  10g caster sugar
  15g cocoa powder

Filling

    800g Cream Cheese

    200g double cream

    1 tin condensed milk

    40g light brown soft sugar

    4 tbsps Ovaltine or Horlicks

    1tsp Vanilla extract

    30g plain flour

    4 eggs

Topping:

    50g Milk Chocolate Spread

    50g Double Cream

    ½ gelatine sheet

    1 packet Maltesers, for decoration

Instructions:

1.Prepare the Biscuits

- Place the digestive biscuits in a food processor and blitz them to fine crumbs.

2. Melt the Butter

- In a saucepan or microwave-safe bowl, melt the unsalted butter.

3. Combine Biscuits, Sugar, Cocoa Powder and Butter

- In the food processor combine the biscuit crumbs with the

caster sugar and the cocoa powder, giving it a brief mix to ensure everything is combined. Add the melted butter to this mixture.

4. Mix Thoroughly

- Blitz the ingredients together for a few seconds in the food processor until the biscuit crumbs are evenly coated with the melted butter, cocoa powder and sugar. The mixture should resemble damp sand.

5. Prepare the Tin

- Take a 9-inch springform tin, which should be sprayed and lined.
- Pour the biscuit mixture into the base of the tin, and spread it out evenly, using a fork. Use the back of a spoon or the bottom of a glass to compact the mixture. Keep the pressure light but firm.

6. Chill the Base

- Place the tin in the refrigerator and let the base chill for 20 minutes or so. This helps the butter solidify, creating a firm foundation for your cheesecake.

7. Preheat the Oven

- Preheat your oven to 160°C.

8. Prepare the Cream Cheese

- In a large mixing bowl, place the cream cheese. Ensure it's at room temperature for smoother blending. If at all possible, buy your cream cheese the day before baking, and leave it out of the refrigerator overnight. Add the double cream to the cream cheese.

9. Add the Condensed Milk

- Open the tin of condensed milk and add it to the cream cheese.

10. Incorporate Sugar and Ovaltine/Horlicks

- Sprinkle the soft light brown sugar into the bowl with the cream cheese and condensed milk. Then add 4 generous tbsps of Ovaltine or Horlicks.

11. Add Vanilla Extract

- Add a teaspoon of vanilla extract to the mixture.

12. Sift in Flour

- Sift the plain flour into the bowl to avoid any lumps in the filling.

13. Blend Smoothly

- Use a hand mixer or a stand mixer to blend the ingredients together. Mix until the texture is smooth and all ingredients are well combined. Ensure there are no lumps.

14. Add the eggs

- Add the eggs, preferably one at a time, and scraping down the sides as you go, ensuring any unmixed ingredients are incorporated into the mix.

15. Pour onto the Base

- Once your chocolate cheesecake base has chilled, pour the cream cheese filling onto it, spreading it evenly, smoothing the top with a spoon.

16. Wrap and Bake

- Wrap the tin in silver foil, then clingfilm, then sliver foil, as per my suggestion in the Bain Marie section of this book.
- Bake at 160°C for an hour, or until golden brown on top but still wobbly in the centre. If you feel it requires longer, give it a little more time in the oven. Once it reaches it's optimum state of being cooked, the cake should 'puff up' above the top of the tin, something that will drop as soon as you take the cake out of the oven.

17. Cool and Chill

- After baking, open the oven door and allow the cheesecake to cool slightly. When ready, remove it from the oven and the Bain Marie, and allow it to cool to room temperature, preferably on a wire rack.
- Cover and refrigerate for at least eight hours, or preferably overnight before preparing the topping.

18. Preparing the topping

- Prepare the Gelatine by soaking the 1/2 gelatine sheet in cold water according to package instructions until it becomes soft and pliable.
- Spoon 40g of Milk Chocolate spread into a glass bowl.
- Heat the mixture over low-medium heat, stirring continuously until the chocolate spread melts. Once this happens, add the 50g of double cream and mix them together.
- Squeeze any excess water from the soaked gelatine sheet and add it to the mixture. Stir until the gelatine dissolves completely, contributing to the setting of the topping.
- As soon as it is ready, pour the mix over the baked and set cheesecake. Do not wait for it to cool! This step ensures a smooth and even distribution of the topping.
- Place the cheesecake with the topping back into the refrigerator to allow it to set completely. This should only take an hour or so, before the cake is ready to serve.

Serve with one or two Maltesers on each slice.

37

REESES PIECES

My Reese's Pieces Cheesecake was a hit from day one at market; a decadent fusion of velvety cheesecake and the iconic flavor of Reese's Pieces peanut butter candies. It has a creamy texture that intertwines seamlessly with the rich and nutty goodness of crunchy peanut butter, all atop a luscious chocolate biscuit base.

Each sumptuous bite is a symphony of smoothness and the distinct taste of Reese's Pieces, delivering a perfect blend of cheesecake luxury and peanut butter delight.

Topped with a chocolate ganache, this dessert is a celebration of sweet and salty, making it a delightful treat for peanut butter enthusiasts and cheesecake lovers alike.

Base

    200g digestive biscuits

    50g salted peanuts, blitzed

    90g unsalted butter

    10g caster sugar

    15g cocoa powder

Filling

  800g Cream Cheese

  200ml double cream

  100g light brown sugar

  100g caster sugar

  200g crunchy peanut butter

  4 eggs

Topping

  1/2 leaf gelatine

  40g Nutella spread, melted

  50g double cream

  Handful Reeces' Pieces for decoration

Instructions:

1.Prepare the Biscuits and the peanuts

- Blitz the peanuts first in the food processor until they are fine like small crumbs. Remove them from the food processor and set them aside for a moment.
- Place the digestive biscuits in a food processor and blitz them to fine crumbs.

2. Melt the Butter

- In a saucepan or microwave-safe bowl, melt the unsalted butter.

3. Combine Biscuits, Sugar, Peanuts, Cocoa Powder and Butter

- In the food processor bowl, combine the biscuit crumbs with the caster sugar and the blitzed peanuts, giving it a brief mix to ensure everything is combined. Add the melted butter to this mixture.

4. Mix Thoroughly

- Blitz the ingredients together for five seconds or so, until the biscuit crumbs are evenly coated with the melted butter, cocoa powder and sugar. The mixture should resemble damp sand.

5. Prepare the Tin

- Take a 9-inch springform tin, which should be sprayed and lined.
- Pour the biscuit mixture into the base of the tin, and spread it out evenly, using a fork. Use the back of a spoon or the bottom of a glass to compact the mixture. Keep the pressure light but firm.

6. Chill the Base

- Place the tin in the refrigerator and let the base chill for 20 minutes or so. This helps the butter solidify, creating a firm foundation for your cheesecake.

7. Preheat the Oven

- Preheat your oven to 170°C.

8. Prepare the Cream Cheese

- In a large mixing bowl, place the cream cheese. Ensure it's at room temperature for smoother blending. If at all possible, buy your cream cheese the day before baking, and leave it out of the refrigerator overnight. Add the double cream to the cream cheese.

9. Incorporate Sugar

- Sprinkle the caster sugar and the light brown sugar into the bowl with the cream cheese.

10. Add the Peanut Butter

- Add 200g of crunchy Peanut Butter to the mix.

11. Blend Smoothly

- Use a hand mixer or a stand mixer to blend the ingredients together. Mix until the texture is smooth and all ingredients are well combined. Ensure there are no lumps.

12. Add the eggs

- Add the eggs, preferably one at a time, and scraping down the sides as you go, ensuring any unmixed ingredients are incorporated into the mix.

13. Pour onto the Base

- Once your cheesecake base has chilled, pour the peanut butter cream cheese filling onto it, spreading it evenly, smoothing the top with a spoon.

14. Wrap and Bake

- Wrap the tin in silver foil, then clingfilm, then sliver foil, as per my suggestion in the Bain Marie section of this book.
- Bake at 170°C for an hour, or until nicely cooked on top but still wobbly in the centre. If you feel it requires longer, give it a little more time in the oven. Once it reaches it's optimum state of being cooked, the cake should 'puff up' above the top of the tin, something that will drop as soon as you take the cake out of the oven.

15. Cool and Chill

- After baking, open the oven door and allow the cheesecake to cool slightly. When ready, remove it from the oven and the Bain Marie, and allow it to cool to room temperature, preferably on a wire rack.
- Cover and refrigerate for at least eight hours, or preferably overnight.

16. Preparing the topping

- Prepare the Gelatine by soaking the 1/2 gelatine sheet in cold water according to package instructions until it becomes soft and pliable.
- Spoon 40g of Nutella into a glass bowl.
- Heat the mixture over low-medium heat, stirring contin-

uously until the Nutella melts. Once this happens, add the 50g of double cream and mix them together.

- Squeeze any excess water from the soaked gelatine sheet and add it to the mixture. Stir until the gelatine dissolves completely, contributing to the setting of the topping.
- As soon as it is ready, pour the mix over the baked and set cheesecake. Do not wait for it to cool! This step ensures a smooth and even distribution of the topping.
- Place the Reece's Pieces chocolates on top of the ganache at regular intervals, allowing the now-setting chocolate hazelnut topping to hold them in place.
- Place the cheesecake with the topping back into the refrigerator to allow it to set completely. This should only take an hour or so, before the cake is ready to serve.

38

LITTLE ENGLISH BREAKFAST

So here's a different take on the humble cheesecake. Embark on a savoury journey with our English Breakfast Cheesecake, a culinary delight that reimagines the classic cheesecake in a savory twist.

This cheesecake is infused with the essence of a traditional English breakfast, featuring flavors of bacon, sausage, mushrooms, tomatoes, eggs, and subtle hints of herbs. Nestled on a hearty oat and herb crust, each delectable bite is a unique symphony of savory goodness.

It's a real celebration of breakfast-inspired indulgence. Perfect for those who crave a savory start to the day, this promises a delightful experience that merges the richness of cheesecake with the comforting flavors of an English breakfast.

And if in doubt: it's like a quiche, only better!

Base

260g savoury oat biscuits

90g unsalted butter

Filling

   1200g Cream Cheese

   4 pork sausages

   6 slices of smoked bacon

   100g button mushrooms, sliced

   100g tomatoes, sliced

   ½ teaspoon of thyme

   Salt and pepper

   45g plain flour

   4 eggs

   50g grated mature cheddar

Instructions

1. Prepare the Biscuits

- Place the savoury oat biscuits in a food processor.
- Pulse the biscuits into fine crumbs.

2. Melt the Butter

- In a saucepan or microwave-safe bowl, melt the unsalted butter.

3. Combine Biscuits and Butter

- In the food processor, combine the biscuit crumbs with the caster sugar. Add the melted butter to this mixture.

4. Mix Thoroughly

- Blitz the ingredients together for a few seconds until the biscuit crumbs are evenly coated with the melted butter and sugar. The mixture should resemble damp sand.

5. Prepare the Tin

- Take a 9-inch springform tin, which should be sprayed and lined.
- Pour the biscuit mixture into the base of the tin, and spread it out evenly, using a fork. Use the back of a spoon or the bottom of a glass to compact the mixture. Keep the pressure light but firm.

6. Chill the Base

- Place the tin in the refrigerator and let the base chill for 20 minutes or so. This helps the butter solidify, creating a firm foundation for your cheesecake.

7. Preheat the Oven

- Preheat your oven to 170°C.

8. Cook the sausages and bacon

- Cook the sausages either under the grill, in a frying pan, or in the oven for half an hour on 200°C.
- Cook the bacon in a frying pan.
- Once both the sausages and bacon are cooked, slice them into small chunks.

9. Slice the mushrooms and tomatoes

- Slice the mushrooms into thin slices. Chip the mushrooms into small chunks.

10. Prepare the Cream Cheese

- In a large mixing bowl, place the cream cheese. Ensure it's at room temperature for smoother blending. If at all possible, buy your cream cheese the day before baking, and leave it out of the refrigerator overnight.

11. Add the sausages, bacon, mushrooms and tomatoes

- Add the sausages, bacon, mushrooms and tomatoes to the mix, and fold them into the cream cheese.

12. Add the Thyme

- Add the Tyme to the cream cheese mix

13. Add salt and pepper

- Add freshly ground salt and pepper to the cream cheese mix to season.

14. Sift in Flour

- Sift the plain flour into the bowl to avoid any lumps in the filling.

15. Blend Smoothly

- Use a hand mixer or a stand mixer to blend the ingredients together. Mix until the texture is smooth and all ingredients are well combined.

16. Add the eggs

- Add the eggs, preferably one at a time, and scraping down the sides as you go, ensuring any unmixed ingredients are incorporated into the mix.

17. Pour onto the Base

- Once your cheesecake base has chilled, pour the cream cheese filling onto it, spreading it evenly, smoothing the top with a spoon. Sprinkle 50g of mature cheddar on top of the cake, ensuring an even spread.

18. Wrap and Bake

- Wrap the tin in silver foil, then clingfilm, then sliver foil, as per my suggestion in the Bain Marie section of this book.
- Bake at 170°C for an hour, or until golden brown on top but still wobbly in the centre. If you feel it requires longer, give it a little more time in the oven. Once it reaches it's optimum state of being cooked, the cake should 'puff up' above the top of the tin, something that will drop as soon as you take the cake out of the oven.

19. Cool and Chill

- After baking, open the oven door and allow the cheesecake to cool slightly. When ready, remove it from the oven and the Bain Marie, and allow it to cool to room temperature, preferably on a wire rack.
- Cover and refrigerate for at least eight hours, or preferably overnight before serving.

Fantastic when served with tomato ketchup!

39

Final Thoughts

It's been a wonderful trip down memory lane, recreating all these delectable delights for you, customers old and new.

I hope that you have as much fun making them as I did creating them, and that you might go further in your kitchen exploits and actually create your own recipes as time goes along. Cheesecakes really are the type of dessert that you can add any flavours to, and it will probably work. They are very much a blank canvas, and so I would encourage you to be brave and try out whatever takes your fancy.

And we had a wonderful seven years creating these cakes and must have made over 10,000 of them during the company's existence.

I wish you all a wonderful baking time. Now I must go to the kitchen, and made a cheesecake or two. Feeling hungry after all that typing!

Sean Jay

2024